UPDATED EDITION

A PLACE OF R

OFFICIAL BOOK OF THE
NATIONAL SEPTEMBER 11 MEMORIAL

EMEMBRANCE

Allison Blais and Lynn Rasic

FOREWORD BY MICHAEL R. BLOOMBERG
108th Mayor of the City of New York
Chair of the National September 11 Memorial & Museum

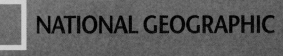

NATIONAL GEOGRAPHIC

WASHINGTON, D.C.

This book is dedicated to the 2,983 men, women, and children killed in the terrorist attacks of September 11, 2001, and February 26, 1993—and to all of their families and friends, so many of whom have worked devotedly and determinedly to help create the 9/11 Memorial and Museum.

May the lives remembered, the deeds recognized, and the spirit reawakened be eternal beacons, which reaffirm respect for life, strengthen our resolve to preserve freedom, and inspire an end to hatred, ignorance, and intolerance.

—FROM THE NATIONAL SEPTEMBER 11 MEMORIAL MISSION STATEMENT

THE MEMORIAL sits at the heart of the rebuilt World Trade Center site (plan, 2011), surrounded by a revitalized lower Manhattan.

CONTENTS

THE MEMORIAL OCCUPIES half of the entire World Trade Center site. Two reflecting pools sit in the footprints of the

twin towers—voids where skyscrapers once stood. The entrance to the 9/11 Memorial Museum is between the two pools.

AT DUSK, the memorial is transformed by light shining up from the pools and through the names of the victims. The

darkening sky is reflected in the glass facades of the museum and surrounding World Trade Center towers.

THE MEMORIAL was dedicated on September 11, 2011—the tenth anniversary of 9/11—in a ceremony for the families of the

nearly 3,000 victims. The next day the memorial opened to the public, and it welcomed one million visitors before the end of 2011.

FOREWORD

The attacks of September 11, 2001, changed our world forever, and they brought loss and grief on a scale we had never known. But the aftermath of the attacks also revealed stories of heroism and sacrifice that inspired us all. They brought us an even deeper appreciation for, and commitment to, our country's founding freedoms. And they brought a powerful sense of unity not just to Americans, but also to people around the world. Out of the ashes of that clear September morning arose what the terrorists could never destroy: hope for a better future, faith in our common humanity, and pride in our country's freedoms and ideals.

The universal impact of the terrorist attacks, and the ethnic and religious diversity of the victims, led people from around the world to offer their support, encouragement, and blessings to our city and country. Many joined Americans from all 50 states who selflessly stepped forward to assist in the unprecedented rescue and recovery. Together with everyone who supported a grieving neighbor, or donated to a charity, or displayed a ribbon or an American flag, we sent a message to the terrorists: We may bend, but we will not break. We may stumble, but we will get back up. Our resilience was so strong because our defiance was so fierce.

This resilience is the true legacy of 9/11. It defined the recovery effort itself, and it is at the heart of the mission of the National September 11 Memorial & Museum. This book chronicles the story of September 11 and the memorial, which is dedicated to the memory of all those killed in the terrorist attacks—in

New York City, at the Pentagon, near Shanksville, Pennsylvania, and in the 1993 World Trade Center bombing. The memorial will be forever a solemn place of reflection and remembrance; we owe that to all those who lost loved ones on 9/11. At the same time, the memorial will forever serve as a reminder of the enormous loss suffered that day, and the enormous sacrifices that were made—and an obligation we owe to future generations.

Family members played a crucial role in the planning and development of the memorial, and it could not have been built without the strong support they have given it. Nor could it have been built without the generous contributions made by people living in all 50 states and 38 countries. Their generosity grew out of the spirit of global unity that emerged in the aftermath of the attacks, and that helped America through some of its darkest hours.

Since the attacks, millions of people from every corner of the globe have visited the World Trade Center site to pay their respects to those we lost. Now they arrive to experience a memorial as beautiful and inspiring as any that has ever been built, which is a testament not only to the creativity of Michael Arad's and Peter Walker's design, but also to the hard work of the memorial staff.

The memories of all those we lost; the courage of all those who saved others; the solidarity that the world showed us; and the resilience that came to define the aftermath of the attacks—all will live on in the memorial and museum, just as they live on in our hearts. And as long as they do, terrorism cannot and will not prevail in our society.

—MICHAEL R. BLOOMBERG
108th Mayor of the City of New York
Chair of the National September 11 Memorial & Museum

INTRODUCTION

September 11, 2001. A date that has come to mean so many things, from horror, pain, loss, and evil to newfound depths of hope, selflessness, generosity, and courage. In the aftermath of devastation, compassion held fast. Around the world, millions watched as the attacks unfolded. The hundreds of first responders rushing into the burning towers and the many civilians helping one another escape revealed the highest levels of fortitude and sacrifice during unthinkable trauma. For months afterward, people reached within themselves for strength and resolve and out to others with profound kindness and support.

The date now also carries the burden of what arose in its aftermath: heightened airport security, the invasions of Afghanistan and Iraq, the 9/11 Commission, the Department of Homeland Security, the illnesses born from working at ground zero, the Navy SEALs' successful operation to kill Osama bin Laden in 2011. This book does not cover that still evolving history. It does offer a glimpse into the pathway of one story: building the nation's 9/11 memorial—from what was destroyed, through the recovery, to the effort to build a lasting tribute to the innocent victims.

Contained within the history of the memorial are countless other stories that helped shaped the creation of America's tribute. This account touches on how designers and planners struggled over construction details and journeys into a few of the lives and relationships now etched as names into the memorial's bronze. It has not been an easy road for anyone involved in the rebuilding—and while this book covers some of the challenges, many are left untold.

We regret that these pages cannot adequately credit the tremendous contributions so many made over the years. From victims' families to government officials, planners, architects, engineers, construction workers, community leaders, and supporters from all over the world, hundreds of thousands have contributed to making this memorial possible. Former New York City Mayor Michael R. Bloomberg, who also serves as the chair of the National September 11 Memorial & Museum, led the city on a path of economic recovery and tenaciously worked toward the realization of the memorial. The Lower Manhattan Development Corporation showed how an unprecedented attack could be met with strength and resilience.

At its core, the 9/11 Memorial's purpose is to honor the people who are no longer with us because a group of Islamist terrorists took them from us far too soon. The memorial also offers a tremendous opportunity to bring people together in much the same way that we saw the world come together immediately following the attacks. For those who may never have a chance to visit in person, we hope this book offers a way of honoring the victims. The act of remembering is a measure of tribute in and of itself.

The 9/11 Memorial Museum is another way to ensure that these men, women, and children are remembered for generations to come. On the wall of the museum between the footprints of the north and south towers, a quote from Virgil, "No day shall erase you from the memory of time," expresses the museum's commitment to honor the memory of the 2,983 lives lost. Emanating from that core mission, the museum serves as the authoritative source for an evolving understanding of 9/11 and its ongoing implications.

The staff of the 9/11 Memorial feel a deep responsibility, having come to know, in some way, those killed, through thousands of stories told so vividly and graciously by their loved ones. May the water, light, bronze, soil, and stone of the memorial help to heal the scar in our city's and nation's heart.

A GLOB

THE TWIN TOWERS each rose 110 stories, becoming landmarks in the New York City skyline. Even before construction

AL ICON

formally concluded in 1973, they became the tallest buildings in the world. The towers soared more than a quarter mile into the sky.

THE TWIN TOWERS had 43,600 windows, but almost all were less than two feet wide, giving the appearance from far away that the buildings were constructed entirely of metal.

1

TWIN TOWERS

AT THE TURN OF THE 21ST CENTURY, the World Trade Center maintained an indomitable presence in New York City. The signature twin towers, rising over a quarter of a mile into the sky, had been fixtures on the city skyline for three decades.

The World Trade Center spanned approximately 16 acres of lower Manhattan real estate and included five buildings in addition to the twin towers, a public plaza, and six belowground levels. The complex hosted more than 430 companies from all over the world in nearly every industry and included a shopping mall, restaurants, a major transportation hub, and government offices.

Approximately 50,000 people worked in the buildings and tens of thousands more visited the complex daily,

either as workers, commuters, shoppers, diners, or tourists. On any given day, the World Trade Center's population equaled that of a small city. In effect, the buildings constituted a city within a city, complete with their own zip code: 10048.

The concept for a world trade center emerged in the late 1950s, when a group of New York business leaders became alarmed by the deterioration of lower Manhattan's position as a commercial hub. The Downtown-Lower Manhattan Association, founded by David Rockefeller, backed the project, which was intended to be the core of a comprehensive urban redevelopment effort to spur economic growth and secure the area's position as a center for global commerce.

A bistate government agency, the Port of New York Authority, which was later renamed the Port Authority of New York and New Jersey, became the builder for the ambitious project, seeing the plan as an opportunity to attract and centralize businesses that would stimulate commerce through the area's ports. Port Authority officials were convinced that the project must be monumental in scale to be fitting of the title "World Trade Center," and to accommodate millions of square feet of new office space for future commercial tenants. The scheme would require a 110-story structure to break the world record for tallest building.

The agency selected the Michigan-based architect Minoru Yamasaki to design a project that would unite a 13-city block area, closing off five through streets and creating a "super block."

VOICES

MINORU YAMASAKI,

Chief Architect of the World Trade Center, 1964

" This great project, to be built in lower Manhattan, for the purpose of bringing together the presently scattered elements of world trade in the most important port in the world, has architectural possibilities which have rarely existed in a project in our times ... Beyond the compelling need to make this a monument to world peace, the World Trade Center should, because of its importance, become a living representation of man's belief in humanity, his need for individual dignity, his beliefs in the cooperation of men, and through this cooperation his ability to find greatness. "

After developing more than 100 designs, Yamasaki and a team of top engineers and architects unveiled a plan for the World Trade Center in 1964. The design called for two soaring towers with clean square tops, sheathed in a gleaming aluminum alloy. To free up as much open office space on the floors as possible, the structures of the towers were built using closely spaced steel columns around the two buildings' perimeters with trusses extending across the floors to a central core. The plan also created room for an innovative elevator system that included 99 elevators in each tower and organized transportation through the buildings like a vertical subway system with local and express elevators that interconnected in "sky lobbies" on the 44th and 78th floors.

At the base of the buildings, Yamasaki's design created gothic arches out of aluminum-clad steel "trees," later known as "tridents." The steel columns

An estimated 1.2 million cubic yards of material were excavated to make room for the foundations of the World Trade Center. The materials were used to expand Manhattan's western shoreline, creating the area known as Battery Park City.

Minoru Yamasaki (opposite) was born in Seattle. The World Trade Center was his architecture firm's first job in New York City.

PLANNING FOR the World Trade Center began in 1960. Plans originally included 5 million square feet of office space

on the east side of Manhattan but eventually came to include 12 million square feet on the west side of the island.

*Escalators (above) carried workers
and visitors to the underground World
Trade Center concourse, which included
a shopping mall and connections to
public transportation.*

*Gothic-style arches (right) ringed the bases
of the twin towers, leading the eyes of a
visitor toward the tops of the buildings, over
one-quarter mile up (opposite).*

converted into three prongs at the top of the lobby level, on the fifth floor, and then continued straight up to the top of each building.

A project of this size, scale, and impact in as dense and diverse a city as New York had its opponents. The future site of the twin towers was "Radio Row," a small cluster of electronics shops, whose owners fought to stop the government takeover of their property. Other detractors included midtown real estate landlords and the "Committee for a Reasonable World Trade Center," led by the owner of the Empire State Building, who took out an ad in the *New York Times* warning of the air traffic safety hazards that the towers would pose to planes as they were flying in and out of New York area airports.

Radio Row merchants waged a fierce legal battle attempting to block the development of the World Trade Center but were ultimately unsuccessful. The Port Authority still had to obtain the approval of the mayor of New York City, however, to put a shovel in the ground.

In 1966, the administration of newly elected Mayor John V. Lindsay did not welcome the surrender of precious lower Manhattan real estate to the Port Authority. To make the deal palatable, the Port Authority proposed using the dirt from the 70-foot-deep excavation that was required to accommodate the giant buildings to enlarge the island of Manhattan and serve as the basis for a waterfront redevelopment project. Originally, the plan had been to dispose of the fill by dumping it into the Atlantic Ocean. Instead, the excavation gave birth to a vast new residential neighborhood: Battery Park City.

With all of the necessary approvals in place, the Port Authority commenced excavation work in August 1966. A massive ditch that became known as "the bathtub" was created to provide the foundation for the towers. The walls of the bathtub required innovative engineering to retain the sides and prevent Hudson River groundwater from seeping into the World Trade Center site.

> I was convinced that the only way to succeed was to build what the *Reader's Digest* called, when I announced the plans in January of '64, the largest building project since the Egyptian pyramids. That was the World Trade Center of New York.
>
> **GUY TOZZOLI**
> FORMER DIRECTOR, WORLD TRADE DEPARTMENT, APPOINTED IN 1962 AND CAREER EMPLOYEE OF THE PORT AUTHORITY OF NEW YORK AND NEW JERSEY

The buildings would sway, believe it or not. If you went into the restrooms on a really windy day, the water in the toilets would actually move back and forth almost like you were on a ship or a boat.

MICHAEL HURLEY

MANAGER, WORLD TRADE CENTER, PORT AUTHORITY OF NEW YORK AND NEW JERSEY

The Windows on the World complex on the top floors of the north tower included an eponymous restaurant, private event space, and a bar called the Greatest Bar on Earth.

A three-foot-thick "slurry wall" was built and held in place by over 1,400 "tiebacks"—cables anchored into bedrock—designed to withstand the constant pressure of the river flowing nearby.

FROM THE OUTSET of the planning process, the World Trade Center's audacious size was the source of both its triumph and its challenge. The towers maintained the title of the tallest buildings in the United States for a mere two years before the Sears Tower in Chicago surpassed them. Critics of the towers found the buildings' size disproportionate to the surrounding locale and inhuman in scale, in part due to the "super block" that eliminated several through streets, creating a division in the area. Others felt that the flat-topped buildings disrupted the gracefulness of the city's skyline. Despite this criticism, the towers managed to find their way into the hearts of many as undeniable icons of New York City, American enterprise and aspiration, and an increasingly interdependent global economy.

An observation deck on the 107th floor of 2 WTC, the south tower, became a favorite tourist attraction that close to two million people visited each year. The deck, what was the highest viewing platform in the world, offered miles of unobstructed views that served as the backdrop for countless tourist photographs. The 106th and 107th floors of the north tower, 1 WTC, were home to the famed restaurant Windows on the World, which hosted weddings, banquets, conferences, and happy hours for downtown workers. Meanwhile, the towers, having become synonymous with New York, were featured in innumerable scenes in movies, television shows, books, and postcards.

In the early years of the World Trade Center, the complex's sheer amount of new, available commercial space meant that the Port Authority did not have an easy time finding tenants. Initially, the Port Authority had intended to attract businesses with commercial interest in the ports and shipping industries. After expanding the marketing efforts to a variety of industries, high-powered companies including investment banks, traders, law firms, and insurance companies finally began to

MAN ON WIRE

PHILIPPE PETIT *called his World Trade Center wire walk* le coup—*the triumph. When the press asked why he did it, he said, "When I see three oranges, I juggle; when I see two towers, I walk."*

On August 7, 1974, a spritely French street performer, Philippe Petit, defied human imagination by walking a high wire between the towers, more than 1,300 feet in the air. After months of planning this incredible feat, Petit spent 45 minutes on a steel cable spanning the 131-foot gap between the towers while police officers waited for him to dismount. Incredulous onlookers over a hundred stories below watched as Petit walked back and forth across the wire eight times. To the delight of the Port Authority's director of the World Trade Department, Guy Tozzoli—who was trying to attract commercial tenants for the buildings—Petit's performance helped boost the public image of the World Trade Center after news of the feat made headlines across the globe.

THE **FORMAL DEDICATION** ceremony for the World Trade Center was held on April 4, 1973, in the lobby of the north

tower. New York Governor Nelson A. Rockefeller called the completion of the project "a dream come true."

You had in this building people from all over the world, all religions, all colors of skin. All everything. All social backgrounds and they lived in harmony. Everybody was very proud to be a World Trade Center tenant, one way or another, working in the World Trade Center. And for me, those flags that were in the lobby of the Trade Center represented a utopia that only can exist in New York.

BRUNO DELLINGER
9/11 SURVIVOR, 47TH FLOOR, NORTH TOWER

move in. By the early 1990s, the World Trade Center was regarded as among the most prestigious commercial real estate in the world. For many, working there meant that they had truly "made it."

■
■

THE COMMERCIAL AND ICONIC success of the World Trade Center also tragically made it a target for terrorism.

On Friday, February 26, 1993, at 12:18 p.m., a small band of Islamist terrorists, with links to a local radical cleric and loosely affiliated with broader terror networks, detonated 1,200 pounds of explosives in a rental van in the underground public parking garage below the southern wall of the north tower. The terrorists fled the garage after manually lighting the bomb's fuse, which killed six people, including a pregnant woman.

Because of wintery weather, many office workers were inside the towers at their desks during the attack, which took place at lunchtime. The

blast shook the towers, partially knocked out power, and created a five-story crater underneath the complex. "I was in pitch blackness, I had nowhere to go," recalled Timothy Lang, who was parking his car in the garage at the time of the bombing. "I only had a sense that I had to get away from that pit because the stuff spewing out of it was killing me and my chest was in pain. So I tried to calm myself. I crawled into a ball into a fetal position and started to pray."

Then director of the World Trade Department for the Port Authority, Charles Maikish recalled that a 14,000-pound piece of steel was blown 100 feet in the air, through a room where four Port Authority employees were having lunch. Massive amounts of water and sewage were seeping into the basement where firefighters and police were conducting searches for survivors, so power was shut off to protect the first responders. As a result, occupants of the buildings became disoriented in the total darkness, and some were trapped in elevators.

As local first responder agencies arrived on the scene, people began evacuating. Black smoke quickly filled the north tower's lobby and began seeping throughout both towers. The dark, smoky conditions in the stairwells made the descent harrowing and slow. In some parts of the buildings, the smoke was so thick that people broke windows to get fresh air. Seventy-two people, including children, were trapped in one elevator for five hours, while dozens of tourists visiting the observation deck, including school groups, waited hours on the south tower roof for the smoke to subside before beginning their descent.

The attack killed six people, including four members of the Port Authority's World Trade Department, an employee of the Windows on the World restaurant, and a visitor to the complex. Hundreds of people required hospitalization for

The February 26, 1993, World Trade Center bombing ripped through five sublevels (above) below the Vista Hotel (3 WTC), near the north tower. Six people were killed and more than a thousand were injured (opposite). It would be over a year and a half before the complex was fully restored.

We all have that feeling of being violated. No foreign people or force has ever done this to us. Until now we were invulnerable.

MARIO CUOMO

GOVERNOR OF NEW YORK, FEBRUARY 26, 1993

their injuries, and many suffered posttraumatic stress from the event.

Although the city was shaken from the attack, tremendous efforts were made so that the lights in the towers were turned on that evening in a show of solidarity and survival.

THE PORT AUTHORITY, under the direction of its executive director, Stanley Brezenoff, worked quickly to repair the damage following the attack. Power and telephone lines were restored, and debris from the bomb's crater was removed. Cleaning crews set to work scrubbing smoke residue off the buildings' walls. The south tower reopened in March, and New York Governor Mario Cuomo and his staff were among the first tenants to return to their office. The entire restoration effort, however, would continue for approximately 18 months.

The bombing prompted a major overhaul of safety and security plans for the complex. The Port Authority invested $250 million in structural, technological, and operational enhancements to help emergency preparedness. New security procedures and notification capabilities were implemented.

Meanwhile, the Federal Bureau of Investigation (FBI) aggressively investigated the attack and succeeded in arresting one of the perpetrators the week following the bombing. Six of the terrorists involved in the plot were subsequently tried, convicted, and given life sentences. One perpetrator remains at large.

A letter that FBI investigators found on the hard drive of one of the culprits, Nidal Ayyad, contained a chilling reminder that the threat against the World Trade Center had not ended. His message stated, "Unfortunately our calculations were not very accurate this time. However, we promise you that next time it will be very precise and WTC will continue to be one of our targets in the U.S. unless our demands have been met."

More than 700 FBI agents were eventually involved in the investigation that followed the bombing. Six of the seven known terrorists behind the attack were convicted and sentenced to life in prison.

AS A NEW CENTURY WAS USHERED IN, the World Trade Center enjoyed success as a global icon. By 2001, the complex's occupancy was at near capacity.

Over a dozen government agencies had offices within the complex. More than 400 firms leased space within the twin towers or other Trade Center buildings, from Bank of America, Metropolitan Life Insurance, and Dun & Bradstreet to Euro Brokers, Inc., Deutsche Bank, and Dai-Ichi Kangyo Trust Company. Banking and finance, insurance, law, import and export, foreign trade, international relations—the array of businesses housed there truly justified the name "World Trade Center." Firms enjoyed the prestige of offices on high floors, such as Cantor Fitzgerald, a bond trading, investment banking, and brokerage services firm that occupied the 101st to 105th floors of the north tower.

Commercial tenants could offer their employees an enjoyable and convenient workplace environment through a number of amenities: direct indoor access

Austin J. Tobin Plaza was sometimes a venue for free concerts and other outdoor cultural programs as part of CenterStage at the World Trade Center.

to an underground concourse, mass transit, dining, shopping, medical and dental offices, postal and shipping counters, full-service banks, meeting and events spaces, and a children's day care center— along with newly enhanced security protocols.

For a growing number of lower Manhattan residents, the World Trade Center became the center of the community. It was where they bought their groceries, ate out, went shopping, and attended public events, including concerts and a farmers market on the plaza. Up above in the north tower, artists worked out of studios provided by the Lower Manhattan Cultural Council.

ON JULY 24, 2001, the World Trade Center complex was transferred by net lease to Silverstein Properties and Westfield America in the richest real estate deal in New York City history. Prior to that time, the Port Authority had operated most of the complex. The $3.2-billion transaction was prompted by the agency's desire to exit the real estate business and focus on its core mission of developing the area's airports, seaports, bridges, and tunnels.

After months of negotiation, Larry Silverstein, president and CEO of Silverstein Properties, told *Real Estate Weekly* that the lease agreement was "a dream come true . . . We will be in control of a prized asset. There is nothing like it in the world."

Just seven weeks later, the rosy future of the World Trade Center would be devastated.

Before September 11, 2001, visitors to the Statue of Liberty (above) could see the twin towers from more than two miles away. After 9/11, the statue closed for security reasons. It reopened in 2009, with a reduced visitor limit to the crown.

Tickets (opposite, above) were required to visit the Top of the World observation deck on the 107th floor of the south tower, one of the few areas in the twin towers open to the public. On a clear day, Top of the World visitors (opposite) could see for 45 miles or more in any direction.

0   **Interior support columns** on the 50,000-square-foot floors of the twin towers.

7   **Buildings** in the World Trade Center.

- 1 and 2 World Trade Center (the twin towers)
- 3 World Trade Center (the World Trade Center Marriott Hotel)
- 4 and 5 World Trade Center (the southeast and northeast plaza buildings)
- 6 World Trade Center (the U.S. Customs House)
- 7 World Trade Center (a 47-story office building)

10   **U.S. Postal Service carriers** delivered mail to the complex every weekday.

16   **Acres of land** occupied by the complex.

22   **Width, in inches, of windows** in the twin towers, selected by architect Minoru Yamasaki because, he said, "People are not afraid of height when the width of the window is not much more than their shoulders."

23.5   **Acres of new land** created through excavation for the World Trade Center, later becoming Battery Park City.

27   **Top speed,** in feet per second, of an express elevator at the World Trade Center.

ER BY THE NUMBERS

Stories in each of the twin towers. `110`

Height, in feet, of the television `360`
mast atop 1 World Trade Center.

Height, in feet, of the `1,377`
World Trade Center observation deck.

Height, in feet, from street level `1,730`
to the top of the television mast.

Workers on the original World Trade `5,000`
Center site during peak construction periods.

Windows in the twin towers. `43,600`

Tons of cooling capacity generated `60,000`
by the World Trade Center's refrigeration plant—
the largest such system in the world.

Cubic yards of concrete used to `425,000`
build the World Trade Center—enough concrete
to construct a sidewalk from New York City to
Washington, D.C.

Square feet of office space in the `12,000,000`
World Trade Center.

Source: Port Authority of New York and New Jersey, 2001.

THE DAY THE W

AFTER AMERICAN AIRLINES Flight 11 crashed into the north tower, many news sources mistakenly reported an accident.

ORLD CHANGED

Not until United Airlines Flight 175 hit the south tower did the world realize the crashes were part of an attack.

BYSTANDERS around the World Trade Center watched in shock as the twin towers burned. Although many fled the area immediately, few realized that the towers would collapse.

2

THAT MORNING

TUESDAY, SEPTEMBER 11, 2001, began as a beautiful, clear day on the East Coast. The public school year had just started. In New York City, polls were open for the primary elections. Tens of thousands of people working at the World Trade Center were headed to their offices. Some were already at their desks.

In Washington, D.C., Congress was in session. The approximately 20,000 military and civilian employees at the Pentagon were starting a new workday.

Millions of households were tuned into the morning newscasts. Flights across the country were in the air or preparing for takeoff. At 7:59 a.m., American Airlines Flight 11 departed from Boston's Logan International Airport bound for Los Angeles.

Within the hour, our world was changed forever.

ON ANY GIVEN DAY IN 2001, tens of thousands of flights departed in the United States. On the morning of September 11, 19 men associated with the Islamist extremist group al Qaeda under the direction of Osama bin Laden boarded four flights intending to hijack the planes and use them as weapons to destroy major American landmarks.

American Airlines Flight 11 carried 76 passengers, nine flight attendants, two pilots, and five of the hijackers. About 15 minutes after takeoff, the plane was overtaken by the terrorists, who stabbed two flight attendants and a passenger.

Two other flight attendants made calls from the coach cabin to report the hijacking to American

I see water. I see buildings. We're very, very low.

MADELINE AMY SWEENEY
FLIGHT ATTENDANT ON BOARD FLIGHT 11

Airlines officials on the ground. One, Betty Ann Ong, stayed on the phone for approximately 25 minutes, calmly reporting from the plane to an American Airlines reservation office in North Carolina. The other, Madeline Amy Sweeney, reached the flight services office in Boston and provided information to help identify the hijackers. As the flight crew worked to keep passengers calm, the plane turned south, descending rapidly. After 45 minutes in the air, Flight 11 approached Manhattan, flying south along the Hudson River. At 8:46, the plane crashed into 1 World Trade Center, the north tower, instantly killing everyone on board and hundreds in the building.

First responders mobilized immediately. News helicopters in the area began reporting the crash, generally presuming an accident had been caused by a small aircraft. Nearby onlookers recalled staring up in disbelief and horror, and seeing the sky fill with white paper blowing out from the tower's gash.

It's getting very bad on the plane—Passengers are throwing up and getting sick—The plane is making jerky movements—I don't think the pilot is flying the plane—I think we are going down—I think they intend to go to Chicago or someplace and fly into a building—Don't worry, Dad—If it happens, it'll be very fast—My God, my God.

PETER BURTON HANSON

IN A PHONE CALL MADE FROM FLIGHT 175, AS REMEMBERED BY HIS FATHER, C. LEE HANSON

UNITED AIRLINES FLIGHT 175 departed Logan International Airport with nine crew members, 51 passengers, and five hijackers. At roughly the same time that Flight 11 struck the north tower, Flight 175 was hijacked. Two passengers and a flight attendant made phone calls to people on the ground, reporting the hijacking. Passenger Brian David Sweeney reached his mother, Louise, and told her that the passengers were considering rushing the cockpit to regain control of the plane. Shortly after 9:00, the plane crashed into the south tower, killing everyone on board and hundreds inside the building.

While Flight 175 was still in the air, American Airlines Flight 77 departed Washington, D.C.'s Dulles International Airport, heading to Los Angeles with 53 passengers, six crew members, and five hijackers. A passenger and a flight attendant reached family members to report the hijacking. At 9:37, the plane crashed into the Pentagon, in Arlington, Virginia. The crash killed all on board and 125 military

The south tower was hit after the north tower, but collapsed first (opposite), only 56 minutes after impact. Flight 175 was traveling at an estimated 560 miles per hour before it crashed.

The news is that it has been hijacked by terrorists. They are planning to probably use the plane as a target to hit some site on the ground. If you possibly can, try to overpower these guys . . . Do everything you can . . . Call me back if you can . . . I love you, sweetie.

ALICE HOAGLAND

IN A VOICEMAIL TO HER SON,
MARK BINGHAM, ABOARD FLIGHT 93

and civilian personnel at the headquarters of the U.S. Department of Defense.

■ ■

MEANWHILE, UNITED AIRLINES FLIGHT 93 en route to San Francisco had departed at 8:42 from Newark International Airport after a 25-minute delay. On board the plane were seven crew members and 37 passengers, including four hijackers.

By 9:00, Federal Aviation Administration (FAA) and airline officials began to piece together that multiple aircraft were involved in the attack. At 9:05, Boston's air traffic center confirmed for the FAA that hijackers on Flight 11 said "we have planes," while the New York air traffic center suspended aircraft departure, arrival, and travel through the New York airspace until further notice. American Airlines ordered a nationwide ground stop between 9:05 and 9:10, followed by a similar order from United Airlines. Conflicting information between the FAA and airline officials slowed down the notification to planes about the hijackings. At 9:25, the FAA Herndon Command Center ordered a nationwide ground stop. Around 9:40, all FAA facilites were given the unprecedented emergency order to instruct all aircraft to land. Air traffic controllers managed to land approximately 4,500 commercial and general aviation planes quickly, without incident.

At 9:19, a United Airlines flight dispatcher began alerting transcontinental flights with a warning to "Beware any cockpit intrusion. Two [aircraft] hit World Trade Center." Flight 93's pilot received the transmission just four minutes before the hijackers attacked the cockpit and took control of the plane.

An air traffic control official in Cleveland and pilots flying in the vicinity of Flight 93 picked up alarming transmissions, including sounds of people screaming. The air traffic controller tried to contact the Flight 93 pilots, with no success. At one point, he heard a voice on the radio: "Keep remaining sitting. We have a bomb on board."

The Pentagon (opposite) is designed as five concentric rings connected by radial corridors. The impact of American Airlines Flight 77 pierced three of these rings and killed 125 people inside.

APPROXIMATELY two billion people, almost one-third of the world's population, are estimated to have witnessed

these horrific events directly or via television, radio, and Internet broadcasts that day.

Twelve of the Flight 93 passengers and crew succeeded in calling loved ones and authorities to report the hijacking. During at least five of the passengers' phone calls, information was shared about the attacks on the World Trade Center by either family members or operators on the ground. This information prompted the passengers and surviving crew members to attempt bravely to overwhelm the terrorists. The hijacker piloting the plane pitched the aircraft downward, trying to throw the passengers off balance. Minutes later, Flight 93 crashed into an empty field near Shanksville, Pennsylvania, killing everyone on board. Yet the passengers did succeed in thwarting a terrorist strike that was presumed to target a Washington, D.C., landmark, most likely the U.S. Capitol Building. Continuing at its last known air speed, Flight 93 would have reached the nation's capital in approximately 20 minutes.

■
■

AS MANY MILITARY AND CIVILIAN OFFICIALS watched the twin towers burning in New York City on television from their offices at the Defense Department, preparing to respond to the attacks, most did not imagine the Pentagon,

with its fortified ringed structure, would be the next target. When Flight 77 barreled into the five-story building, witnesses saw a fireball created by the jet fuel, which erupted 200 feet above the roof. The plane penetrated three of the Pentagon's five rings. The combination of the jet fuel and the architecture of the building created an inferno-like situation that some survivors had to escape. Later in the afternoon, the impact zone of the west facade, known as the Pentagon's E ring, collapsed as first responders fought to put out the fires.

"I was blown through the air. When I landed I didn't know where I was . . . The room was just black and everything I touched burned my hands . . . I remember seeing strings from my hands that were just hanging off the burns," recalled John Yates, Army civilian security manager, about the blast.

Immediately, first responders who arrived on scene put a search and rescue operation together with military personnel. Five triage areas were set up outside the building to help victims, many badly burned and needing medical attention.

Defense Department Secretary Donald Rumsfeld, who had been in his Pentagon office at the time of the crash, also joined the search and rescue effort on the lawn of the Pentagon. Officials later observed that the casualties could have been worse had the plane not struck a newly renovated part of the building where some offices were still unoccupied and windows were fitted with blast-resistant glass.

ON A TYPICAL WEEKDAY, between 16,000 and 19,000 people arrived at the World Trade Center by 8:45 a.m. That morning, employees of Risk Waters Group, a London-based business services firm, were helping restaurant employees set up for a conference at the north tower's Windows on the World on the 106th floor. Hundreds were expected; about 80 had arrived. At the insurance broker-age and risk management firm Marsh & McLennan, more than 200 people were starting their workday on the 93rd through 100th floors. In the five floors above that, where the bond trading firm Cantor Fitzgerald was headquartered, 658 employees were already in the offices or reporting into work.

At 8:46 Flight 11 crashed into the 93rd through the 99th floors of the north tower at about 495 miles an hour. All three emergency stairwells were sev-ered. A fireball exploded, starting fires on several floors. Hundreds were trapped above the impact zone. Evacuation below was hindered by jammed

United Airlines Flight 93 crashed in a field outside Shanksville, Pennsylvania (opposite), after passengers tried to wrest control of the plane from its hijackers. Debris from the plane was later found up to eight miles away from the site of impact.

Fires at the Pentagon (above) burned for days after September 11. Debris from Flight 77 landed as far as 1,000 feet from the building.

doors and debris-filled stairwells. Others were trapped in elevators. Minutes after arriving on the scene, fire department officials decided that the fire raging in 1 WTC was so powerful that it could not be fought. First responders began heading up the stairwells of the building, with the primary mission now to rescue and evacuate. At 9:03, the unimaginable catastrophe confronting the first responders doubled as a second aircraft barreled into 2 WTC.

After the north tower had been hit, an announcement came through the public address system in the south tower stating that "Building 2 is secure." Many who had worked in the building in the 1993 attack began an immediate evacuation. When the Port Authority broadcasted evacuation orders approximately seven minutes after the first announcement, thousands of south tower occupants had already started vacating the building. Less than one minute after the evacuation notice, Flight 175 ripped through the 77th to the 85th floor of the south tower, severing two of the three emergency stairwells. As in the north tower, people were trapped inside elevator cars, while some on floors above the impact zone had little way of escaping. An enormous fireball erupted, seen from Brooklyn to New Jersey. The sight of the two towers billowing with

Each of the hijacked flights on 9/11 carried as much as 11,400 gallons of jet fuel when it left the airport. The explosions in the twin towers roared through the elevator shafts, spreading fire far from the impact floors.

VOICES

KEATING CROWN,
9/11 survivor, 100th floor, south tower

"A number of the elevator doors had been blown off. Fire was coming up through the shaft. It was just very difficult to see. There was not much sound ... There were a couple of other people calling out to try and help or find someone. Ceilings collapsed and marble walls crumbled. It was unclear which direction to go. I vaguely knew where exits were on the floor, but . . . in this type of thick, black smoke, it's totally impossible to see those exit signs. So, I ducked down, was crawling at times, fell a number of times. As it turns out I had a broken leg and other pretty severe cuts and lacerations to my body . . . I ran into a colleague and we decided to go down. As we were about to turn and go down, another colleague of ours, a woman was calling out our names. We turned around. I started to pick her up and put her on my back. My colleague said, 'Keating, we have 78 flights to go, you're not going to carry her down.' So we carried her between us as if we were carrying her off a football field or a sporting event."

First responders offered masks and water to people in the World Trade Center vicinity as they evacuated. Across the country, sites like Disney World, the Golden Gate Bridge, and major government offices were also cleared.

The FDNY (opposite) dispatched over 200 units to the World Trade Center on 9/11. After the collapse of the south tower, the incident commander and his team moved toward Chambers Street to the north, but they returned to the site soon after and were killed when the north tower fell.

black smoke erased any notion that the catastrophe had been caused by accident. America was under attack.

Within minutes of the second crash, first responder agencies mobilized additional personnel to help manage the crisis, which included evacuating people safely through falling debris and shattered glass. Firemen carrying as much as 56 pounds of protective gear and firefighting equipment ascended the stairs of the two towers as streams of civilians made their way down.

"When the firefighters came . . . they were panting, they were breathing heavily, sweating profusely . . . some people gave them our water to drink and we poured water on their heads to cool them down. As they proceeded up the

I noticed the cuffs of my pants were on fire . . . I started digging and I heard someone say "Don't leave me."

TOM CANAVAN
9/11 SURVIVOR, WHO WAS TRAPPED ON
THE CONCOURSE LEVEL BELOW THE TOWERS

stairs, we applauded them," recalled Manuel Chea, who worked in the north tower on the 49th floor.

Some people trapped in the towers called 911 for help. Others dialed family members to say that they loved them. Callers reported unbearable smoke and heat conditions in the upper floors. People huddled together in conference rooms, and others, desperate for fresh air, broke windows. Generally, 911 operators and fire department dispatchers instructed callers to remain where they were and wait for firefighters—standard advice emergency officials recommend when responding to high-rise fires. "As we got very close to the World Trade Center . . . things were falling around us . . . I realized that I saw a man, it wasn't debris, that I saw a man hurling himself out of the 102nd, 103rd, 104th floor . . . I was in shock . . . I said to the police commissioner that we're in unchartered territory, we've never gone through anything like this before," New York City Mayor Rudolph W. Giuliani said to the 9/11 Commission.

Despite worsening conditions, first responders mounted stairs, searching floors for survivors. Meanwhile, civilians in the towers also helped in the rescue effort, freeing occupants trapped behind collapsed walls and jammed doors. Some carried the injured down dozens of stairs. The many heroics of rescue personnel and civilians will never entirely be known, but it is certain that thousands of lives were saved because of their brave and selfless acts.

VOICES

BEVERLY ECKERT,

in a StoryCorps interview, remembering her conversation with her husband, Sean Paul Rooney, minutes before the collapse of the south tower

"It was about 9:30 a.m. when he called. He told me he was on the 105th floor and he'd been trying to find a way out . . . I asked if it hurt for him to breathe and he paused for a moment and then said 'no.' He loved me enough to lie. We stopped talking about escape routes and then we just began talking about all the happiness that we shared during our lives together. I told him that I wanted to be there with him—die with him. But he said, 'No, no.' He wanted me to live a full life. As the smoke got thicker he just kept whispering 'I love you' over and over. I just wanted to crawl through the phone lines to him and hold him one last time. I heard a sharp crack, followed by the sound of an avalanche. It was the building beginning to collapse. I called his name into the phone over and over and then I just sat there pressing the phone to my heart."

In the south tower, one stairwell remained intact, the only means of escape from above the impact zone. Only 18 people are known to have navigated their way through the smoke-filled, debris-congested stairwell from floors within or above the impact zone. Moments after they escaped, the tower collapsed, creating an explosion so gigantic that the southern tip of Manhattan became enveloped in a massive dust cloud. People on the surrounding streets ran from the debris, choking on dust, ducking into buildings, and diving under cars. The collapse caused seismic waves observed in five states and up to 265 miles away.

Following the south tower collapse, the chief of the New York City Fire Department (FDNY), Peter James Ganci, Jr., ordered all units to evacuate the north tower and moved the department's command post farther north. After burning for 102 minutes, the north tower collapsed at 10:28 a.m. Less than two hours after the first jet hit, the World Trade Center had vanished in a giant cloud of dust and smoke plumes.

Ganci, along with FDNY First Deputy Commissioner William M. Feehan and over 300 members of the FDNY, perished on the morning of September 11. Their colleagues continued battling raging fires throughout the day. Fires had spread to surrounding buildings, including 7 WTC, which stood across the

The north tower (above) collapsed in less than 12 seconds at 10:28 a.m., killing hundreds of people instantly. No one from above the north tower impact zone survived.

Father Mychal F. Judge (opposite), chaplain of the FDNY, was killed when the south tower collapsed. Thousands attended his funeral on September 15, 2001.

THE TOWERS' COLLAPSE coated the streets and buildings of lower Manhattan in gray dust. It would be weeks—

for some, more than a year—before many residents could return home to their damaged apartments.

THE SURVIVORS' STAIRS

Hundreds fled to safety using a stairway on the north side of the World Trade Center that connected the elevated plaza to Vesey Street below. Kayla Bergeron, director of media relations for the Port Authority on 9/11, was evacuating from the north tower when the south tower collapsed. When she emerged from the building, the Vesey Street stairs were the closest passage for her to escape from falling debris on the plaza. Bergeron later described the stairs as being the "path to survival and to freedom." At the end of the recovery and cleanup effort at ground zero, the stairs that had become known as the "Survivors' Stairs," became the last aboveground remnant of the original World Trade Center. Recognizing their historic significance and symbolic meaning to survivors of the attacks, officials decided to preserve the flight of stairs and incorporate them into the National September 11 Memorial Museum.

THE VESEY STREET STAIRCASE *remnant weighs 58 tons. It was installed in the future 9/11 Memorial Museum site in July 2008.*

street from the twin towers. First responders monitored neighboring buildings that might be in danger of collapsing. In the late afternoon, the 47-story 7 WTC was the last tower to collapse. Intense fires had eroded its structural stability. There were no casualties because the building had already been evacuated. Through mountains of burning rubble, twisted steel, and detached rebar at the World Trade Center, which would soon be known as ground zero, search and rescue teams worked all night to locate survivors.

BY THE LATE MORNING of September 11, America's largest city and the world's financial capital was nearly shut down. Mayor Giuliani, who had been in the vicinity of the World Trade Center with FDNY Commissioner Thomas Von Essen and other city officials, escaped the collapse of the south tower on foot and ordered the evacuation of lower Manhattan. City Hall and other government offices, located just blocks from the World Trade Center, had been evacuated, and he needed new headquarters from which to operate city government. Swaths of downtown were without power and phone service. Schools had sent children home. Entry into the borough of Manhattan was halted, and service on

On September 11, a number of the city's public subways halted service, and thousands left Manhattan on foot. For more than a week after September 11, the Brooklyn Bridge was closed to all traffic except emergency vehicles.

This mass terrorism is the new evil in our world today. It is perpetrated by fanatics who are utterly indifferent to the sanctity of human life and we, the democracies of this world, are going to have to come together and to fight it together and eradicate this evil completely from our world.

TONY BLAIR

U.K. PRIME MINISTER, SEPTEMBER 11, 2001

President George W. Bush boarded Air Force One in Florida around 9:54 a.m. on September 11. Less than 12 hours later, he addressed the nation on television from the White House.

many public transportation lines was interrupted. Thousands made their way across bridges to Brooklyn and Queens, while others walked northward up Manhattan's avenues.

New York Governor George E. Pataki suspended state primaries and mobilized the National Guard. In Washington, D.C., the Capitol Building and the West Wing of the White House were evacuated. Vice President Richard Cheney moved to a sheltered conference room, accessed by a tunnel under the White House. President George W. Bush, who had been visiting a school in Florida when he learned of the attacks, was moved aboard Air Force One as a security measure.

Major American destinations such as Walt Disney World in Orlando, the Sears Tower in Chicago, and the United Nations in New York were evacuated. All commercial planes remained grounded in the first-ever national emergency ground stop of aircraft. The Centers for Disease Control and Prevention in Atlanta prepared to respond to the threat of bioterrorism. The Defense Department declared Force Protection Condition Delta—the highest level of alert. From Norfolk, Virginia, the military deployed battleships and the Air Force began combat air patrols over major cities on the East Coast. The country braced itself for further attack.

As evening fell, fires continued to burn at the World Trade Center. All seven buildings in the complex and a number of surrounding buildings were fully destroyed or irretrievably damaged. In one day's time, an area roughly the size of 12 American football fields had become a smoldering chaos. The Empire State Building was once again the tallest building in the New York City skyline, and it remained unlit that night in a display of mourning.

That day, an estimated one-third of the world's population watched the events unfold on television or saw news reports of the attacks. Political and religious leaders across the globe joined in denouncing the attacks. Both allies of the United States and those hailing from countries historically unfriendly to the American government, including Libya, Cuba, and Iran, issued public messages expressing their condolences. President Bush returned to the White House, and that night, he addressed a shaken nation. Speaking directly into the camera from the Oval Office, he said, "These acts of mass murder were intended to frighten our nation into chaos and retreat. But they have failed. Our country is strong. A great people has been moved to defend a great nation."

The attacks resulted in nearly 3,000 fatalities—the largest loss of life from a foreign attack on American soil. The oldest victim was 85 years old; the youngest was two and a half. Victims included nationals from over 90 nations and practitioners of every major world faith. First responders perished heroically. The FDNY lost 343 members plus three retirees, the Port Authority Police Department lost 37, and the New York City Police Department lost 23— the largest loss of emergency responders in a single event in U.S. history.

Many firefighters remained on site to aid rescue efforts, which began immediately, went on through the night, and continued for weeks. Fires at the site burned as hot as 2000°F and made conditions there treacherous and exhausting.

TIME LINE OF EVENTS

7:59 AM   **American Airlines Flight 11,** Boston to Los Angeles, takes off from Logan International Airport with 76 passengers, 11 crew members, and 5 hijackers on board.

8:14 AM   **United Airlines Flight 175,** Boston to Los Angeles, takes off from Logan International Airport with 51 passengers, 9 crew members, and 5 hijackers on board.

8:20 AM   **American Airlines Flight 77** takes off from Washington Dulles International Airport, en route to Los Angeles with 53 passengers, 6 crew members, and 5 hijackers on board.

8:42 AM   **United Airlines Flight 93** takes off from from Newark International Airport, en route to San Francisco with 33 passengers, 7 crew members, and 4 hijackers on board.

8:46 AM   **Hijackers deliberately crash** Flight 11 into floors 93 through 99 of the north tower (1 WTC).

8:54 AM   **While flying** over southern Ohio, Flight 77 turns to the south without authorization.

BY 9:00 AM   **The Fire Department of New York** (FDNY), the New York Police Department (NYPD), and the Port Authority Police Department (PAPD) mobilize at their highest levels.

9:03 AM   **Hijackers deliberately crash** United Airlines Flight 175 into floors 77 through 85 of the south tower (2 WTC).

9:37 AM   **Hijackers deliberately crash** American Airlines Flight 77 into the Pentagon, near Washington, D.C.

SEPTEMBER 11, 2001

The FAA orders all civilian planes in U.S. airspace to land and prohibits departures. Approximately 4,500 planes must land at the nearest airport. | 9:42 AM

Evacuations begin at the White House and U.S. Capitol, where the House of Representatives and Senate are in session. | BY 9:45 AM

The south tower (2 WTC) collapses. | 9:59 AM

After learning of the other attacks, passengers on United Airlines Flight 93 launch a counterattack on hijackers aboard their plane to try to seize control of the aircraft. In response, the hijackers crash the plane into an empty field in Pennsylvania. | 10:03 AM

The north tower (1 WTC) collapses. The 16-acre WTC site is in ruins, with collateral damage affecting all adjacent properties and streets. A rescue and recovery effort begins immediately. | 10:28 AM

NYC Mayor Rudolph W. Giuliani orders the evacuation of all civilians in lower Manhattan below Canal Street. | 11:02 AM

Mayor Giuliani holds a press conference with New York Governor George E. Pataki and other public officials at the New York Police Academy, a temporary headquarters for city offficials. When asked the number of victims, Giuliani says, "The number of casualties will be more than any of us can bear, ultimately." | 2:35 PM

7 WTC collapses. | 5:20 PM

President George W. Bush addresses the nation. | 8:30 PM

FROM RESCUE

SOME OF THE Gothic arches that once characterized the twin towers survived their collapse. Each shorn column

TO RECOVERY

panel weighed more than 100 tons, some swaying dangerously in the wind.

INITIALLY, RESCUE WORKERS avoided bringing machinery into the unstable site. Instead they formed bucket brigades, passing bucketfuls of debris from person to person as they searched for survivors.

3

GROUND ZERO

WITHIN HOURS OF THE ATTACKS, thousands of New Yorkers and millions of people across the country and around the world felt compelled to respond to the crisis. Lines of donors formed outside blood banks. Community groups started impromptu drives for goods and money to help victims' families and survivors. With air traffic suspended, medical staff from Dallas, Texas, drove across the country to provide 70 square feet of skin grafts for Pentagon burn victims. In Gander, Newfoundland (population 10,000), residents offered food, clothing, and housing to nearly 7,000 stranded passengers from flights diverted to their local airport. Volunteer firefighters, emergency medical technicians, trained relief workers, and spontaneous volunteers from counties and states that neighbored the three crash sites rushed to help in the recovery efforts.

Ground zero itself was sort of like the magnet. People got up and they said I've got to be there . . . We set aside our egos . . . our titles . . . we set aside whatever it is that makes people think they're different, and we decided to work together.

RONALDO VEGA

NYC DEPT. OF DESIGN AND CONSTRUCTION
PROJECT MANAGER DURING RECOVERY

The Federal Emergency Management Agency (FEMA) arrived in New York on September 12, to aid search and rescue efforts and investigate the buildings' collapse.

At ground zero, 2,700 vertical feet of structural materials had been compressed into a mountainous, smoldering pile of scraps of steel, splinters of concrete, tangled rebar, and unrecognizable gray material. The wreckage burned at temperatures reaching 2000°F. The air was thick with dust and smoke and the overwhelming stench of burnt rubber, plastic, and ashes. Despite the toxic conditions, rescue workers, now joined by ironworkers, carpenters, electrical workers, and other volunteers, continued to search for survivors through the night of September 11.

In the early hours of the aftermath, workers used picks, axes, shovels, and, when tools were not available, their bare hands to uncover pockets under the debris where people might still be alive. Bucket brigades of hundreds of people snaked through the ground zero pile. Every step on the unstable surface was made more hazardous by fires that burned beneath the rubble.

Eighteen people were pulled alive from the wreckage after the towers fell on September 11, 2001. The hope of finding more survivors fueled the exhausted workers and made the search all the more frantic. By the morning of September 12, an estimated 5,000 people had converged upon the pile to help in the search. At 12:30 p.m., 30-year-old Genelle Guzman was freed from the rubble after being buried for more than 26 hours. She was the last survivor found at ground zero.

AT THE PENTAGON, firefighters worked to extinguish fires, hampered by smoke, debris, unstable walls, and the threat of addtional terrorist attacks, including reports of an incoming aircraft. Federal Emergency Management Agency (FEMA) search and rescuers from Maryland, Virginia, and Tennessee

A rescue dog (above) named Gus from Tennessee waits to enter the wreckage at the Pentagon.

The windows in the World Financial Center (left) were blown out, but the buildings remained standing and structurally sound.

worked together with the Arlington County Fire Department and the military to find survivors, while others stabilized structures to prevent additional damage and injuries to the rescue workers. The only survivors from the attack were those who escaped the building's fiery wreckage immediately after the crash.

In Somerset County, Pennsylvania, state police, federal officials, volunteers, and local emergency workers flooded the strip-mined field where Flight 93 crashed. The plane's impact created an enormous crater and torched surrounding trees and acres of earth. The force of the crash had plunged the fuselage deep into the ground. Investigators recovered the plane's flight data recorder a couple days after the crash, and later found the cockpit voice recorder buried 25 feet below the ground's surface. Federal Bureau of Investigation (FBI) and coroner's office officials, forensic archaeologists, and other investigators combed the site and surrounding area for human remains. In the weeks and months that followed the crash, remains for every victim on board Flight 93 were found and identified.

> If you didn't know, you would have thought no one was on the plane. You would have thought they dropped them off somewhere.
>
> **WALLACE MILLER**
> **SOMERSET COUNTY CORONER**

Excavating machinery with claws called grapplers rolled around the site throughout the recovery effort. Before grappler operators could remove steel debris from the site, ironworkers weakened and cut the steel with hand torches.

IRONWORKERS WERE AMONG THE FIRST of the thousands of volunteers who came to ground zero. Their union, Local 40, had helped build the twin towers, and now they were tasked with removing the remnants. Their expertise in cutting and handling steel proved crucial to the effort. A number of building and construction trade members and first responders on site had connections to the World Trade Center or knew someone who was missing in the pile.

People came to ground zero not just to help at the site, but to support the recovery workers putting in strenuous shifts. American Red Cross and Salvation Army staff and volunteers were joined by medical personnel, chiropractors, podiatrists, and others who set up relief centers all around the site. St. Paul's Chapel, where George Washington once worshipped, transformed its pews into stations where workers were able to rest, eat meals, and receive medical attention and counseling.

"The spirit of what happened in this space turned everybody into volunteers, turned everybody into relief workers in some sense," said Diane Reiners, relief coordinator for St. Paul's Chapel.

Workers were confronted daily with horrific evidence of death and violence. Even the most seasoned first responders and construction workers had never seen anything remotely close to this level of destruction from a fire or demolition job. They faced enormous challenges, not the least of which were the hazards of operating machinery on the precarious pile. Concerns over erecting

A group of mostly retired firefighters sometimes called the "Band of Dads" participated in the recovery, hoping to find the bodies of their missing sons. Most left with nothing, but all refused to leave until the end of the recovery efforts nine months later.

VOICES

HALE GURLAND,
sculptor, photographer, and volunteer rescue worker, in an NPR interview, 9/14/2001

"You want to find these people. It's an emergency . . . You want to see if you can find more alive people, so you don't really think about it . . . You don't think about the twisted metal and about your hands and that you're hurt because . . . it could be you under there. I think it's humanity at its best, and before it was humanity at its worst . . . And just to stand there and to see what once was a building, especially in that smoke. It's a war, and it's never going to be the same."

BY SEPTEMBER 12, an estimated 5,000 workers had converged at the site, motivated by the belief that survivors were

trapped in the rubble. Ultimately, only 18 people emerged from the debris alive, 14 of them together in one stairwell.

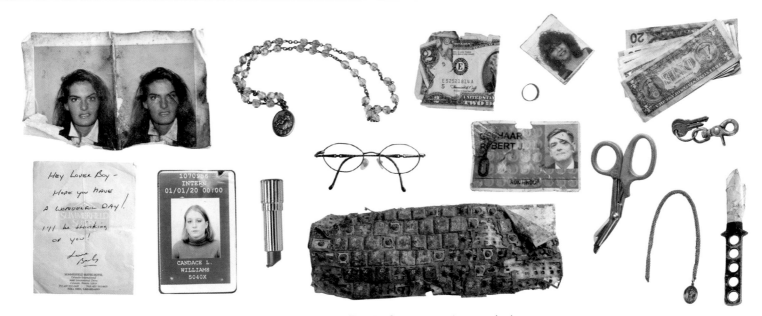

cranes and using heavy machinery within the World Trade Center perimeter led to the use of excavators known as grapplers. The machines' caterpillar tracks enabled them to roll over any terrain and keep their weight distributed. The grapplers, equipped with hydraulic arms and a claw, could perform the essential tasks of nimbly picking up material and hauling multi-ton steel columns.

Compounding the dangers at ground zero was the unknown stability of the World Trade Center's slurry wall—a three-foot-thick retaining wall that kept the waters of the Hudson River from flooding the site. Supporting the over 3,000-foot-long, 70-foot-high wall were bundles of cables called tiebacks, as long as 150 feet and bolted into bedrock. Engineers helping to survey the damage on site feared the demolished buildings now filling the World Trade Center's foundation were the only reason the walls had not collapsed. A breach in the slurry wall could flood the area and undermine surrounding buildings. Extricating wreckage would have to be done cautiously to make sure the wall was not ruptured before it could be reinforced.

To facilitate the removal of material from ground zero, the City of New York reopened the Staten Island Fresh Kills facility, which was formerly a landfill and was later slated to become parkland. Working with the NYC Department of Sanitation and other local, state, and federal agencies, the NYPD and FBI painstakingly combed through the rubble for any criminal evidence, personal effects, and human remains. Within just three days of the attacks, an estimated 1,500 truckloads filled with 9,000 tons of material had been transferred to Fresh Kills.

The FDNY (opposite) lost hundreds of firefighters from units all over the city. In total, more than 400 first responders were killed. All were posthumously awarded the 9/11 Heroes Medal of Valor by the White House.

Thousands of individual objects (above) were discovered amid the World Trade Center debris, everyday items like ID cards and computer keyboards that came to symbolize the magnitude of what—and who—had been lost.

The New York City Department of Design and Construction (DDC) was designated as the agency that would manage the cleanup of the site. DDC split the site into four "quadrants" and divided the work between four major construction management companies, enabling the agency to manage operations in a more organized way. In such physically and emotionally taxing circumstances—hundreds of people at times were working with little sleep—tensions frequently flared at the site. Construction workers, firefighters, members of the Port Authority and New York City Police departments, DDC officials, and the contractors differed over how best to manage the recovery effort while expeditiously and safely moving debris.

INITIALLY AFTER 9/11, the NYPD created a frozen zone stretching from the southern tip of Manhattan north to 14th Street, restricting access to all except

The New York Stock Exchange never opened on September 11—a Tuesday—and remained closed until the following Monday. First responders joined Mayor Giuliani and New York Senators Charles Schumer and Hillary Clinton for the opening bell ceremony on September 17.

emergency personnel. The West Side Highway, which runs adjacent to the World Trade Center site, was closed to traffic to clear the way for rescue workers and heavy machinery en route to assist in the recovery effort. Subway and train service remained suspended in parts of lower Manhattan due to damage caused by the World Trade Center collapse and to prevent further harm to fragile city infrastructure. Utility companies sought to restore electricity and phone service to downtown.

Bomb scares rattled city residents and workers. Midtown offices emptied out into the streets as heavily armed police officers with bomb-sniffing dogs responded to reports of suspicious packages. Mayor Giuliani urged New Yorkers not to overreact, saying, "People have to understand we are living with a great deal of faith here. Remain calm." Fearing the attacks would cripple the economy, returning the city to a sense of normalcy was of paramount importance to government officials and business leaders. Wall Street fulfilled a pledge to resume stock trading on the Monday following 9/11. Mayor Giuliani reopened City Hall for business that same day in a show of resolve and solidarity. Meanwhile in Washington, D.C., New York's Senators Charles E. Schumer and Hillary Rodham Clinton worked with U.S. Representative Jerrold Nadler (whose district included the World Trade Center) and others from the New York congressional delegation to secure federal funds to rebuild.

Despite efforts of city, state, and federal officials to restore lower Manhattan, it would be weeks and months—over a year in some cases—before thousands of evacuated residents could return to their homes downtown. A number of apartments sustained extensive damage such as blown-out windows, ash-filled living rooms, clothing coated in dust, and furniture singed by fire. Displaced residents lived in temporary housing, some for months on end, others for over a year. The catastrophe also caused the temporary closure of seven downtown public schools, displacing thousands of students. Two schools and a community college campus near the World Trade Center site were commandeered by the Red Cross and emergency management officials as outposts.

"We didn't know if we were ever going to see the inside of our home again . . . so you really had the feeling that whatever you took might be the only material remains of your life—that sentimental life . . . the family recipes, my grandmother's wedding rings . . . the stuff that you can't replace. So, we left with whatever we could take on our backs," said Kathleen Gupta, a resident of lower Manhattan.

The windows of stores downtown, some city blocks away from the towers, shattered as the towers fell. Merchandise inside became laden with dust.

You'd relieve another unit. They would go home and you would report. You would just start your digging and searching. Sometimes you would find somebody. Sometimes you found a friend.

FDNY LT. MICKEY KROSS (RET.)
9/11 SURVIVOR, ONE OF 14 TO SURVIVE TOGETHER
IN A PIECE OF NORTH TOWER STAIRWELL

Businesses in the area struggled to keep their doors open. Delis, restaurants, clothing stores, shoeshine shops, and other small businesses—particularly those closest to ground zero—suffered crippling losses of revenue. Thousands of people lost jobs. Economic development officials with New York City and state sought to assist small businesses while also trying to retain large companies considering moves to midtown, New Jersey, Long Island, and Connecticut. Some businesses held steadfast and stayed in lower Manhattan, whereas others found new locations or permanently closed.

THE RECOVERY WORK WAS COMPLEX, dangerous, grueling, and fraught with emotion. Hopes of finding survivors waned. By early October, Mayor Giuliani declared that the work at the site had shifted from being a rescue operation to one that focused on recovering the remains of the dead and removing the wreckage of the buildings. The intense recovery effort continued into 2002, under the direction of Mayor Michael R. Bloomberg, who succeeded Giuliani in January.

The search for human remains was intensely personal for workers on the pile. A group consisting mostly of retired firefighters known as the "Band of Dads," spent months at the site hoping to find the bodies of their missing first responder sons. On December 11, 2001, retired firefighter Lee Ielpi retrieved the body of his son, Jonathan Lee Ielpi, a firefighter. Jonathan was one of only 176 victims whose whole bodies were recovered relatively intact.

The New York City Office of Chief Medical Examiner remained on standby to receive any human remains that were found. They had been on site since the very beginning. On September 11, Dr. Charles Hirsch, the chief medical examiner, had responded to the catastrophe at the World Trade Center and himself sustained injuries. He remained on the spot nonetheless, ready to help cope with the staggering number of casualties.

Nearly 18,000 small businesses (opposite) were destroyed, displaced, or forced to shutter after 9/11. The volatile economic environment that followed resulted in nationwide layoffs that affected nearly 130,000 employees.

Missing posters (left) lined New York City, bearing the faces of men and women who would eventually be declared victims of the attacks at the World Trade Center.

VOICES

ROSEMARIE O'KEEFE

Commissioner of the mayor's Community Assistance Unit from 1996 to 2001

"We needed to give [the victims' families] some kind of token because most of them didn't have anything to bury. They didn't have a gravesite to visit ... [The mayor] asked me to create an urn, a box, something ... We came up with something round and out of wood with a little brass nameplate that they could inscribe later, we placed it in a very sturdy black box and we presented it at the pier to each family member with an escort with an American flag in a private room. And one gentleman just took it out and held it up ... and he said, 'This is my wife. This is what I have of my wife. And this is what I will treasure the rest of my life.'"

The Port Authority Police Department, charged with protecting the property of the Port Authority of New York and New Jersey—including New York City's main bridges, tunnels, and airports—lost 37 of its officers on 9/11.

The relatives of the missing reeled from unspeakable losses. To help victims' loved ones, assistance centers were set up in New York, New Jersey, as well as in other states with concentrated numbers of family members, such as Massachusetts. Mayor Giuliani set up a family assistance center at Pier 94 on the Hudson River. From grief counseling to legal assistance, the center attempted to offer every service that the families could possibly need. The city encouraged family members to submit materials belonging to their loved ones, such as combs and toothbrushes, to help the medical examiner collect comparison DNA samples for the missing.

As the recovery effort wore on, the realization that many bodies might never be recovered took hold. Due to the compression and tremendous heat from the violent plane crashes and the ensuing fires, recovering and identifying human remains proved difficult. In late October 2001, the city distributed urns filled with ashes from ground zero as an offering of solace and condolence to the families.

Workers at the site resolutely persisted in their efforts to find whatever remains they could, even small fragments and tiny bones. The search would continue even after the official end of the recovery operation. In 2006, Mayor Bloomberg ordered a new search for remains at and near the World Trade Center, including

BEAM OF HOPE

THE STEEL BEAM *and column that came to be known as "the cross" stood on-site as a symbol of faith and resilience for many involved in the recovery efforts.*

Construction worker Frank Silecchia found a fused steel column and beam among the rubble of 6 World Trade Center on the evening of September 13, 2001. Many saw the 17-foot-tall artifact as a cross. In early October, it was moved to the edge of the site, where it was more visible and accessible to workers and the public. The cross was blessed by Father Brian Jordan, a Franciscan priest who had been ministering to workers and blessing human remains recovered at the site. Father Jordan conducted Mass and offered Communion at the base of the I-beam cross Sunday after Sunday. "It didn't matter what religion you were, what faith you believed in," said Richard Sheirer, commissioner of the Office of Emergency Management at the time. "It was life, it was survival, it was the future."

THE NYPD lost 23 officers on 9/11. After the attacks, Commissioner Raymond Kelly spoke of "the enduring example

they leave us: the example of what it means to stand courageous in the face of evil."

on the rooftops of surrounding buildings, after Consolidated Edison workers discovered remains. Deputy Mayor for Operations Edward Skyler, who oversaw the expanded search, said that "even if the result had been only one more remain or one more piece of personal property, it would still have been well worth it."

Since 2001, over 21,800 human remains have been found and given over to the medical examiner for identification. While the remains of 40 percent of the victims have not been identified, the medical examiner continues to maintain a repository of remains, hoping to identify them as DNA technology advances.

Amid such an unprecedented recovery process, some family members were deeply concerned that remains of their loved ones were being overlooked during the sorting process at Fresh Kills. A group of families petitioned and eventually lost a lawsuit to require the removal of more than one and a half million tons of ground zero material to a burial site.

To many victims' relatives, the World Trade Center was the final resting place of their loved ones. The tragedy made sacred the very footprints of the towers where so many innocent lives had been lost. A movement driven by family members to preserve the footprints would later emerge as an overwhelming force in determining the future of the World Trade Center and shaping a vision for the memorial.

Many items found in the pile were returned to owners or families. Others, like a firefighter helmet broken into three pieces (above), were so badly damaged that ownership could not be determined and instead fell into the care of museums or other agencies.

On May 30, 2002, the official end of recovery operations at ground zero, an empty stretcher was ceremoniously carried out of the site (opposite) in honor of the more than 1,100 victims for whom no remains were found.

BY THE SPRING OF 2002, the 70-foot-deep hole was emptying rapidly, and the recovery and cleanup effort was coming to a close. It is estimated that in just under nine months, 3.6 billion pounds of debris had been removed from what some began referring to as "the pit" through an estimated three million hours of steadfast labor. Tens of thousands of people took part in the effort—including volunteers who came from all over the country.

On May 28, workers gathered in the excavated site to cut down the "Last Column." The 36-foot-tall, 58-ton piece of steel was a core column of the south tower. Adorned with graffiti tributes inscribed by first responders and construction and recovery workers who had participated in the grueling ground zero operations, the column was the last remaining upright vestige of the skyscrapers. Two days later, the column, shrouded in black, was removed from the site in a ceremony marking the official end to the recovery. Hundreds of first responders and workers lined the ramp leading out of the pit and saluted the column as it left the site.

While the job at the site had ended, many workers contended with lingering emotional and health effects. Thousands of rescue and recovery workers and other people who lived and worked near the World Trade Center continue to suffer from a range of physical and mental health problems. According to medical findings, more than 11,000 firefighters who responded on 9/11 experienced at least one new respiratory symptom within a week of the attacks. Thousands continue to suffer from conditions including what is known as the "World Trade Center cough." Others have reported acute breathing problems, worsening asthma, post-traumatic stress disorder, cancer, and other illnesses requiring sustained treatment. In many ways, workers who contributed to the herculean recovery effort have had to endure their own recovery from 9/11.

TIME LINE OF RES

9.12.2001   **At 12:30 p.m.,** rescuers searching the north tower wreckage locate Genelle Guzman. She will be the last of 18 people to emerge from the rubble alive.

9.13.2001   **Structural engineers** begin examining the structural integrity of buildings on the periphery of the World Trade Center site.

9.17.2001   **Professional construction** and credentialed recovery workers take over the operations at ground zero. Volunteers continue to assist in the effort.

9.28.2001   **More than 134 tons of material** have been removed from the site; NYC Mayor Giuliani estimates that the cleanup will take "anywhere from nine months to a year."

10.6.2001   **The last federal rescue team** leaves ground zero. Although workers hope to find survivors, their official mission shifts to recovery.

10.8.2001   **Workers discover** a fault line adjacent to the slurry wall encircling the World Trade Center site. Engineers are concerned it might rupture, causing flooding that would compromise recovery operations and potentially affect areas of lower Manhattan. The slurry wall remains a concern throughout the recovery effort.

10.28.2001   **A memorial service is held** at the World Trade Center site for victims' families.

10.30.2001   **New York City officials** announce plans to cut the number of uniformed personnel at the site. Out of the approximately 150 FDNY firefighters and NYPD and PAPD officers on duty at the site, 25 from each agency would remain in order to return staff to their regular assignments in the city.

CUE TO RECOVERY

At least **$200 million** worth of gold and silver is removed from a Bank of Nova Scotia vault under 4 WTC. — **10.31.2001**

Firefighters protest plans to scale back their presence on site. Eventually the city allows 75 firefighters to remain. — **11.2.2001**

New York Governor Pataki states that the FDNY has extinguished the fire at the World Trade Center site. FDNY remains on standby in case small pockets of fire or "hot spots" are discovered. — **12.19.2001**

Trapped Port Authority Trans-Hudson (PATH) train cars are removed from the World Trade Center site. — **2.20.2002**

The six-month anniversary of the attacks is marked with "Tribute in Light," an art installation projecting two shafts of light upward from lower Manhattan. — **3.11.2002**

Construction workers cut down the "Last Column," the final standing column of the World Trade Center. — **5.28.2002**

The column is removed from the site in a public event attended by thousands, ceremonially marking the end of the recovery and cleanup operations. — **5.30.2002**

The last truckload of debris is carried out of the World Trade Center site. — **6.25.2002**

THE IMPULSE T

America America land of hap...
freedom rings from every
From sea to sea!

We the people of the United States in order to form a more...
the general welfare, and secure the bles...
this constitution f...

I pledge allegiance to the flag
of the United States of
... and to the
O... America...
... one nation...
indivisible with liberty
and justice for...

God Bless A...

O MEMORIALIZE

Pier 94 Family Assistance Center in New York City. The center closed in 2002, but the banner was saved.

SPONTANEOUS MEMORIALS cropped up all over the world. One emerged in Union Square, at the border of the "frozen zone" south of 14th Street, where solemn crowds continued to gather for weeks after the attacks.

4

NEVER FORGET

Along with the urge to help at the World Trade Center site, the instinct to memorialize was spontaneous worldwide. With nearly 3,000 people killed, there were tens of thousands of victims' family members; estimates of between 25,000 and 50,000 survivors who had been in or near the towers during the attacks; and countless more who had lost friends or colleagues. Even those who did not know anyone who perished wanted to ensure the victims did not become mere statistics. The act of memorializing victims, scholar Edward Linenthal has said, "is a protest, a way of saying, 'We will not let these dead become faceless and forgotten.'" That spirit of remembrance infused the world's immediate response to 9/11.

This is a journey that, in a sense, began within moments of the attack—with the first flower laid gently on the steps of Trinity Church, the first candle to flicker in Union Square Park, the first heartfelt message inscribed on the viewing platform overlooking ground zero.

KEVIN M. RAMPE
LMDC PRESIDENT (2003–2005) AND LATER
CHAIRMAN (2006–2007)

Many New Yorkers gravitated to Union Square, long a magnet for public gatherings in celebration and in sorrow. Because 14th Street, the square's southern border, was the northern edge of the "frozen zone," it was a natural choice for those looking to mourn together. Within a day, continuous vigils to honor the victims began, and the park was lined with candles, photographs, flags, letters, poems, and children's drawings.

Around the city, the front doors of firehouses and police stations became shrines, and first responders left the lockers of those who had fallen as they were, uniforms hanging and personal effects just as they had been on the morning of 9/11. New Yorkers paused in front of "Missing" posters plastered on surfaces throughout the city,

The first responders who were killed spent their final moments as heroes, struggling to save others. Firehouses and police stations across the city quickly filled with tributes to their bravery and sacrifice.

searching the faces of those who were gone. As hope for rescue faded, many of those posters were transformed into memorials themselves, sewn into quilts and pasted onto murals and sculptures.

Memorial services allowed all Americans opportunities to gather together— from the National Day of Prayer and Remembrance at the National Cathedral in Washington, D.C., and A Prayer for America service at Yankee Stadium, to the tens of thousands of simple candlelight vigils in town squares and other public settings across the nation.

Thousands of relatives of missing loved ones visited a dedicated view- ing platform at ground zero itself. They were joined by countless others at another platform nearby—people who may not have lost anyone they knew, but who needed to see up close what they had witnessed from afar and pay their respects. The platforms, erected in late 2001, were adorned with flowers,

In December 2001, a temporary viewing platform (above) opened to the public just north of the ruined World Trade Center site. As with the firehouses, visitors quickly covered it in tributes and mementos.

FREEDOM QUILTS

WHEN BETTY NIELSEN *first felt compelled to create quilts for the families of 9/11 victims, she set out to make five. She didn't imagine that in three months, backed by a team of volunteers, she would deliver 1,500 quilts to New York.*

Betty Nielsen of Fonda, Iowa—population 750—decided to organize her community to make quilts for families who had lost loved ones. "In my heart I felt so strong that I could not just let this go," Nielsen recounted. "I went to my church's Altar Society and pleaded my case, asking them each to make a block for a quilt to give to a family of a victim, and it was overwhelming how everybody said yes." By the time Nielsen left for New York to deliver the quilts around Christmas, she had 1,500 of them. She called the project "Freedom Quilts" and gave them out to families at the Family Assistance Center at Pier 94 with the slogan: "Made with love to comfort you."

patches of uniformed officers, and expressions of sympathy, quickly becoming living memorials of the tremendous compassion so many felt.

An organization called ArtAID created a "Wall of Remembrance" to line the platforms, listing every victim's name interspersed with images of tribute left at the site—including a fireman's prayer, letters from children, and a simple note: "With deepest gratitude in honor of the police officer who saved our son's life on September 11, 2001. We do not know your name. We hope you survived. Please know that we are eternally grateful." At the end of the recovery effort, the wall was dismantled and moved to the Union Square subway station.

THE TRAGEDY ALSO SPURRED a widespread impulse to create tributes humble and elaborate. Donors from around the world sent what they could to the family assistance centers at Pier 94 in Manhattan and Liberty State Park in New Jersey.

As teachers struggled to find a way to address with children what happened on 9/11, many spearheaded projects that allowed their students to express their sympathy to New Yorkers. Students at the Porter-Gaud Lower School in Charleston, South Carolina, created a 12-foot-wide length of cloth, which brightened the walls of the children's play area of the Family Assistance Center.

Thousands attended the multifaith Prayer for America service held at Yankee Stadium (left) on September 23, 2001. In the season after the attacks, the Yankees and other Major League Baseball teams adopted "God Bless America" as the song played during the seventh-inning stretch.

The day after 9/11, recovery workers at the Pentagon unfurled an enormous American flag (above) over the side of the building in honor of President George W. Bush's visit to the site. One month later, it was lowered with full military honors.

MISSING POSTERS were initially created with hope that survivors would emerge from the rubble, but as recovery

at the site wore on, the posters became their own memorials to those who were not missing, but gone.

The "Forever Tall" mural (right), created by CITYarts, graced the side of 35 Cooper Square in New York's East Village until 2004. Painted by student artists, the mural showed flowers filling the twin towers on the Manhattan skyline.

The Statue of Liberty fiberglass replica (opposite) that appeared outside an FDNY firehouse came to be known as Lady Liberty. The collage of tributes that cover it includes handmade paper cranes and United Airlines wings pins.

VOICES

TANYA HOGGARD

Delta Airlines flight attendant and keeper of the "Dear Hero" collection

"I was grounded in Paris on September 11th. When I finally got back to the United States seven days later, I needed to do something—anything—to help. I volunteered at ground zero where I found myself hanging up letters from children that had been sent directly to first responders—from as far away as Australia, France, Pakistan, and all 50 states. The massive quantity was overwhelming, and I learned from some of the firemen that they were running out of space in the firehouses. Ironically, all of the paper was becoming a fire hazard! They would have to start throwing it away.

I decided I could save them. These materials told the story of 9/11 through the eyes of children. So, I took my suitcase, filled with duffel bags, and began the yearlong journey of collecting these letters and pictures and brought them all back to my house . . . trip after trip. I wasn't sure what I'd do with it all, but I knew this moment in history had to be preserved. Ultimately I compiled nearly three tons of material. And I called it the 'Dear Hero' collection—because most of the letters started with that simple yet uplifting phrase, 'Dear Hero.' "

High school students and community residents, organized by CITY-arts, created a mosaic mural on the side of a building in Manhattan's East Village. Called "Forever Tall," the artwork restored the twin towers to the Manhattan skyline, built with a mosaic of flowers.

Other memorial tributes were more spontaneous, like the fiberglass replica of the Statue of Liberty that FDNY Lt. Robert Jackson found one morning outside his firehouse, which had lost 15 men in the attacks. Lady Liberty, as the firehouse would come to call her, was soon covered from torch to toe in tributes left by passersby from around the world—a flag made of children's blocks, another with a paper towel roll flagpole, ribbons, origami cranes, uniform patches, Mass cards, rosary beads, condolence notes, and angel figurines.

Many Americans experienced a powerfully renewed sense of patriotism, and the display of American flags multiplied exponentially to the point that many flagmakers found themselves temporarily out of stock. Expressions of sympathy poured into the United States from around the world, many of them taking the form of large projects inviting broad participation. One, organized by the Internet French Beaded Flower Group, asked individuals around the world to make beaded glass flowers to be used in memorial wreaths for the three attack sites. Stem after stem arrived from far-flung countries including Australia, Italy, France, Canada, and Switzerland.

Outside the site of the Flight 93 crash in Somerset County, Pennsylvania, hundreds of spontaneous remembrances were brought and left behind. Like Union Square, the crash site became a gathering place for those seeking to mourn and pay their respects.

At the Pentagon, a decision was made to preserve an original block of masonry charred by the fires with the inscription "September 11, 2001," to be relaid in its original location when the building was restored, less than one year after the attack.

THE URGE TO MEMORIALIZE was accompanied by an equally powerful need to rebuild at the World Trade Center site. In November 2001, the Lower Manhattan Development Corporation (LMDC)

The entire nation has embraced New York, and we have responded by vowing to rebuild our city—not as it was, but better than it was before.

FROM THE LMDC'S BLUEPRINT
FOR THE FUTURE OF LOWER MANHATTAN (2002)

A model created by the Lower Manhattan Development Corporation (above) showed the stark blank space where the World Trade Center had been—a space that would be home to a new master plan for the rebuilding.

"Tribute in Light" (opposite), a pair of powerful light beams that shone into the Manhattan skyline, became a powerful icon after 9/11.

was established as a subsidiary of the Empire State Development Corporation to plan and coordinate downtown's rebuilding and revitalization. Governor Pataki named John C. Whitehead the agency's chairman. A self-described "child of the Depression" from Montclair, New Jersey, Whitehead had landed at Normandy on D-Day, led Goldman Sachs during the rise of investment banking, served as former President Ronald Reagan's deputy secretary of state, and chaired numerous nonprofit institutions. As LMDC chair, his charge was to build the agency from the ground up. Louis R. Tomson, a former first deputy secretary to Governor Pataki, was hired as the agency's first president.

With the leadership of the city's congressional delegation, the federal government granted $2.8 billion to the LMDC through the U.S. Department of Housing and Urban Development, dedicated to revitalizing downtown.

The core of the LMDC's efforts was to plan a permanent memorial that would honor all of those killed, while simultaneously creating a vibrant plan for rebuilding the World Trade Center site as a whole. Extending outward from there, with downtown's residential vacancies soaring and businesses swiftly relocating, the agency prioritized attracting and retaining residents and businesses, restoring transportation, and improving the quality of life throughout lower Manhattan. Looking back on the early days of planning years later, John Cahill, Governor Pataki's secretary and chief of staff, recalled, "In the days, weeks, and months after September 11, there was a spirit of unbreakable solidarity, irrepressible optimism, and unprecedented unity. It was that spirit that sustained us and was the driving force behind all of our efforts downtown."

One of the LMDC's first actions was to create a "Blueprint for the Future of Lower Manhattan," a document to guide the process of developing and evaluating plans for a memorial and the creation of a vibrant, mixed-use community in lower Manhattan. The plan emphasized the need for public involvement throughout the process. Over the next few years, the LMDC held more than 200 public meetings, carried out extensive outreach to victims' families, and received tens of thousands of comments from around the world.

VOICES

JOHN C. WHITEHEAD

Chairman of the Lower Manhattan Development Corporation from 2001 to 2006

"That terrorist act was a challenge against what the United States stood for. All our principles of human rights and human freedoms were challenged, and we had to have a strong response that would honor the victims of the tragedy but also help restore our standing in the world . . . We had to be ready to build things that were beautiful and respectful. And we had to be proud of how we rebuilt, and what it would look like when it was finished . . .

We wanted it to represent what the public wanted, as we should in a democracy, so we declared a period of public listening. Many people will remember that famous July meeting at the Javits Center when 5,000 people turned out to vote, and they turned down all our options for rebuilding the site. They didn't accept any of them. So we went back to the drawing board, had some new people involved, a new competition, and more plans. And as a result I think we had the right plan in the end."

Fritz Koenig's 25-foot-tall sculpture "The Sphere" resided on the World Trade Center plaza before 9/11. Koenig began working on the piece in his barn in Bavaria; its bronze segments were assembled in Germany and it was shipped whole to the United States.

On September 11, 2006, former mayor of New York City Rudolph Giuliani (opposite) stood before a reflecting pool at ground zero filled with flowers, as a participant in the commemoration ceremony to those who had been lost five years before.

To ensure discussion among all of the constituencies affected by the agency's work, several advisory councils were formed. The Families Advisory Council in particular, whose members consisted entirely of 9/11 victims' relatives, became highly involved in the process to develop the memorial and museum.

WHILE PLANNING FOR a permanent memorial was under way, officials unveiled plans for an interim memorial. Fritz Koenig's "The Sphere," a 45,000-pound sculpture, had adorned the fountain on the World Trade Center's plaza from 1971 to 2001. Bent and damaged, but still recognizable, the sculpture would be installed in Battery Park and unveiled on the six-month anniversary of the attacks. On the same day in March 2002, the "Tribute in Light" would soar over lower Manhattan for the first time. Illuminating the night sky on September 11 every year thereafter, the "Tribute in Light" beams quickly became a symbol of endurance and hope, uniting those directly affected by the attacks with people from around the world witnessing the glowing skyline.

The LMDC also continued to support memorial efforts through a number of projects led by Anita Contini, its senior vice president for memorial, cultural, and civic programs. StoryCorps launched an initiative to record the memories of victims' family members, responders, and survivors. Family organizations called September's Mission and Voices of September 11th created the Living Memorial, an online initiative to gather remembrances for each of the victims. And in 2006, the September 11th Widows' and Victims' Families Association created the Tribute Center, a powerful space for exhibits and educational purposes to tell the story of 9/11 and the days that followed.

With almost no buildable land left in Manhattan, the 16 acres at ground zero constituted some of the most valuable real estate in New York City. At the same time, the site was imbued with emotion and loss, and had become a spiritual place for people around the world. The challenge of what to build on a site of such complications—in terms of both meaning and physical infrastructure—was immense.

It now has a different beauty—one I could never imagine. It has its own life, different from the one I gave to it.

FRITZ KOENIG
CREATOR OF "THE SPHERE"

THE FLIGHT 93 crash site in Somerset County, Pennsylvania, became a place of tribute for thousands of Americans.

Forty angels decorated with flags appeared along the site's edge, one for each of the flight's crew and passengers.

Opinions diverged wildly on what should fill the void created by the twin towers. Some advocated that the towers be immediately rebuilt; others likened the site to a sacred burial ground, asking that it remain empty.

Most wanted a memorial, but the question of how big it should be and how much of the World Trade Center site constituted "hallowed ground" was hotly debated. Many wanted to rebuild the towers in a show of strength and indestructibility. Others thought the entire 16 acres should remain empty with no development whatsoever. Local residents wanted a regular street grid to be reintroduced to the site rather than creating another super block. Commuters called for public transportation; community advocates asked for affordable housing. Commercial and retail space, a new home for the New York Stock Exchange, a garden, a school, a hospital, a library, a museum, a religious center, a center for world peace—each had its advocates.

The local community board, U.S. Representative Jerrold Nadler, and New York State Assembly Speaker Sheldon Silver helped to ensure an open dialogue between downtown residents and the agencies involved in the rebuilding. In July 2002, through a process led by the LMDC's urban planner, Alexander

Garvin, six preliminary concept designs were unveiled for the 16-acre site. The LMDC hoped the concepts would spark a public dialogue that would guide planners on the path to a master plan for the most important redevelopment project in New York City history. The concepts were presented at a series of public forums, and in July 2002, the LMDC and the Port Authority sponsored an event created by the Civic Alliance to Rebuild Downtown New York, a broad-based coalition of over 85 groups. Titled "Listening to the City," this 21st-century version of a town hall meeting was held at the Jacob Javits Convention Center in Manhattan. About 4,500 people (and another 800 joining online) participated in the largest public urban planning dialogue in history.

Strangers sat together at tables and talked about where they were during the attacks and what they thought about the future of New York. Participants were given remote voting devices to respond instantly to polls held throughout the day. Looking out over the crowds, Whitehead remarked, "This is what the terrorists didn't understand. This is what they didn't know. It's absolutely beautiful."

Although the participation was inspiring and 96 percent of those there said they were satisfied with the dialogue, their responses to the six concept plans were the opposite. Dan Doctoroff, NYC's deputy mayor for economic development and rebuilding, told the press, "If I had to sum up what I heard today in one phrase, it would clearly be: Don't settle. Do something great."

Heeding the clear call from the public, officials decided to scrap the initial concept designs and launch a worldwide competition for a new master plan for the World Trade Center site.

THE LMDC received 406 submissions from around the world, from which a panel of architectural and planning experts selected seven of the most innovative teams. Those teams then produced nine designs, unveiled in December

I couldn't come in with a shovel and a pair of gloves—but this has allowed me to do something, however small, to express my love and support for New York City and the victims.

PARTICIPANT
"LISTENING TO THE CITY," JULY 2002

The 4,500 people who attended "Listening to the City" were placed in small groups of 10 to 12, seated at round tables. Attendees of all ages, races, and income levels were present—one in five self-identified as a 9/11 survivor.

The Libeskind plan promises to add an element of modern vision and magnificence to the already striking New York City skyline. These buildings will stand proudly as living reminders of New Yorkers'—and Americans'—strength and resilience for decades to come.

GEORGE E. PATAKI
GOVERNOR OF NEW YORK, FEBRUARY 2003

2002. About eight million people visited the plans online, and the LMDC received nearly 13,000 comments. Designs by two teams, THINK (an architect team including Shigeru Ban, Frederic Schwartz, Ken Smith, and Rafael Viñoly) and Studio Daniel Libeskind, were selected as finalists. Both concepts were further developed, and in February 2003, "Memory Foundations" by Studio Daniel Libeskind was announced as the winner.

Libeskind's plan reconciled the strong impulses both to preserve the World Trade Center site and to rebuild the skyline. The plan included a tower—the tallest in the country at 1,776 feet—at the northwest corner, which Libeskind called the Freedom Tower. A series of smaller towers spiraling downward in height encircled a memorial, appearing to protect and embrace it. The memorial site included the footprints of the twin towers themselves, and, key to Libeskind's vision, allowed a portion of the slurry wall that held back the Hudson River during the attacks to remain visible as a symbol of the strength and durability of democracy.

Libeskind also included new cultural facilities, which would come under a great deal of scrutiny in the years to follow. Another important component of the plan was the new World Trade Center Transportation Hub, which the

VOICES

DANIEL LIBESKIND

Statement on the World Trade Center Master Plan, 2002

"When I first began this project, New Yorkers were divided as to whether to keep the site of the World Trade Center empty or to fill the site completely and build upon it. I meditated many days on this seemingly impossible dichotomy. To acknowledge the terrible deaths which occurred on this site, while looking to the future with hope, seemed like two moments which could not be joined. I sought to find a solution which would bring these seemingly contradictory viewpoints into an unexpected unity. "

famed Spanish architect Santiago Calatrava would later design to resemble a bird in flight. In late 2003, the LMDC brought in architect David Childs to design the Freedom Tower.

THE MASTER PLAN left open the footprints of the twin towers for a memorial, to be designed through an international competition. The tributes to the 9/11 victims that had burst forth around the world made clear the need for a central memorial at the very site where the attacks had taken place—the ground made sacred through tragic loss. And so the master plan for the World Trade Center left a place for such a memorial at its heart.

Studio Daniel Libeskind's winning master plan received worldwide attention. Matthew Higgins of the LMDC managed the crush of media as the new vision for the World Trade Center was unveiled to the public.

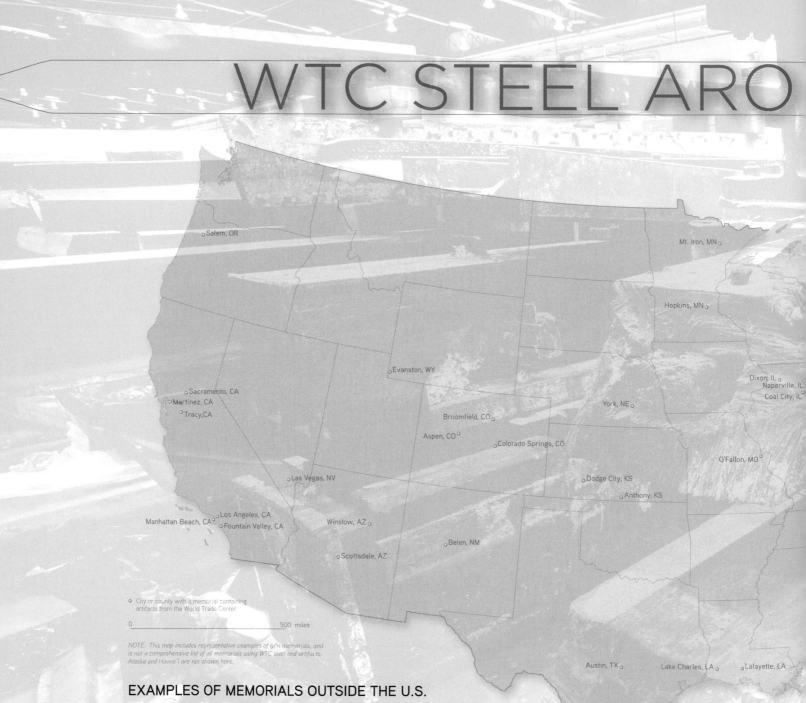

WTC STEEL ARO

Salem, OR

Mt. Iron, MN

Hopkins, MN

Dixon, IL
Naperville, IL
Coal City, IL

Evanston, WY

Sacramento, CA
Martinez, CA
Tracy, CA

York, NE

Broomfield, CO

Aspen, CO

Colorado Springs, CO

O'Fallon, MO

Las Vegas, NV

Dodge City, KS

Anthony, KS

Manhattan Beach, CA   Los Angeles, CA

Winslow, AZ

Fountain Valley, CA

Belen, NM

Scottsdale, AZ

○ City or county with a memorial containing
artifacts from the World Trade Center

0   500 miles

NOTE: This map includes representative examples of 9/11 memorials, and
is not a comprehensive list of all memorials using WTC steel and artifacts.
Alaska and Hawai'i are not shown here.

Austin, TX   Lake Charles, LA   Lafayette, LA

EXAMPLES OF MEMORIALS OUTSIDE THE U.S.

Bagram, Afghanistan
Christchurch, New Zealand
Eilat, Israel
Jerusalem, Israel
London, England
Padua, Italy

Portland, MI
Lansing, MI
Eastlake, OH
Westerville, OH
Potsdam, NY
DeWitt, NY
Clifton Park, NY
Portland, MI
New York
100 miles
Ocean City, MD
Charlottesville, VA
Norfolk, VA
Salem, VA
Jacksonville, NC
Moody, AL
Windermere, FL
Palm Beach Gardens, FL

EXAMPLES OF MEMORIALS WITHIN 100 MILES OF NEW YORK CITY

Atlantic Highlands, NJ	Harrison, NJ	Shrewsbury, NJ
Basking Ridge, NJ	Haverstraw, NY	Smithtown, NY
Buena Vista, NJ	Howell, NJ	Somerville, NJ
Chatham, NJ	Jersey City, NJ	Stirling, NJ
East Meadow, NY	LaGrange, NY	Stony Point, NY
Edison, NJ	Lincroft, NJ	Summit, NJ
Farmingdale, NY	Livingston, NJ	Union County, NJ
Garfield, NJ	Lower Makefield, PA	Union Vale, NY
Glen Gardner, NJ	Madison, NJ	Wethersfield, CT
Glen Rock, NJ	New York, NY	Woodbridge, NJ
Great Neck, NY	Parsippany, NJ	
Green Brook, NJ	Setauket, NY	
Greenport, NY	Sewell, NJ	

A GLOBAL MEMORIAL

The City of New York and the Port Authority of New York and New Jersey made available to the public about 2,000 pieces of World Trade Center steel for 9/11 memorials around the world. About 200 of these pieces belong to the National September 11 Memorial & Museum at the World Trade Center. Others now make their homes worldwide, appropriately representing the international impact of the attacks. Some weigh tons, and others are more intimate pieces. A letter requesting steel stated, "It's a small piece of steel to fill our big hearts." One memorial is not tied to a specific place on this map: the U.S.S. *New York,* whose bow was built with seven and a half tons of steel debris from the World Trade Center. "America always comes back," Secretary of the Navy Ray Mabus said at the ship's commissioning in November 2009. "That's what this ship represents." The museum tracks 9/11 memorials throughout the world through an online registry that is a testament to the global impact of 9/11 and the diverse ways in which individuals and communities have continued to remember the attacks.

ENVISIONING

THE DESIGN for the memorial was chosen from more than 5,000 entries, including finalist "Passages of Light: Memorial

THE MEMORIAL

Cloud" by bbc art + architecture, in which a crystalline cloud of light represented a dressing over a wound.

WHEN ARCHITECT Daniel Libeskind envisioned the new World Trade Center master plan, he imagined One World Trade Center would recall the torch of the Statue of Liberty.

5

MANY VISIONS

IN THE MASTER PLAN that defined the World Trade Center site, roughly half of the 16 acres was reserved for a memorial. Yet what constituted an appropriate memorial was unclear. People eloquently expressed hopes that the space would reflect the deep wounds New Yorkers, the nation, and the world had suffered. Others argued the memorial should emphasize not grief but rather the resilient spirit that emerged in the days following the attacks. Or both, as one "Listening to the City" public forum participant said: "The essential message is that we have suffered losses but we survive these events and we go on."

Even a question that seemed simple—"For whom are we creating the memorial?"—elicited a multitude of responses.

Nothing we do, of course, will ever replace what we lost that tragic day. But by choosing a fitting memorial, we can honor the lives, spirits, and the courage of our loved ones.

PAULA BERRY
MEMORIAL JUROR WHOSE HUSBAND, DAVID, WAS KILLED IN THE SOUTH TOWER

"Everyone who died. Everyone who survived. Everyone who helped," said one participant in the "Listening to the City" forum. "For all of us, for everyone who needs to heal," said another.

"For the nation, for New York, and for New Yorkers." And another: "For the World Trade Center itself and what it stood for as a symbol of our global village."

Because memorial planning began so soon after the attacks, emotions remained intensely raw, with searing grief infused into every discussion. The task was immense: to create a place that could be instilled with that loss while also expressing the love and compassion that had arisen from it—one that would have an impact strong enough to reach future generations.

MANY IDEAS OFFERED in initial public discussions about creating the memorial drew predictably from already existing memorials: a wall of names, a monumental statue. Other proposals were new: two flagpoles the height of the twin towers, a bell to toll at the moments the planes impacted the towers.

In the fall of 2002, members of the LMDC and its advisory councils toured memorial sites in New York City and around the country to learn about their successes and challenges. They visited the great memorials on the National Mall in Washington, D.C., the National Law Enforcement Officers Memorial, and the Oklahoma City National Memorial, along with others both well and lesser known, from abstract to literal, from vast in scale to intimate.

Vietnam Veterans Memorial Fund President and Founder Jan Scruggs explained the mission statement that had guided the design competition he had organized, which declared that the design must include all 57,000+ names of soldiers missing or killed, be apolitical, be harmonious with the site, and facilitate a healing process. Entries were judged by a jury of art professionals, and Scruggs said they were able to see the power of Maya Lin's submission immediately through very simple sketches. Since Lin's selection in 1981, he noted, memorial design competitions had become more popular around the world.

Reminding the group of the Vietnam Memorial's highly contentious development period—and the critical acclaim and public embrace of Lin's design at its end—Scruggs advised them, "Controversy will accompany any truly meaningful process." It would be a repeated theme. Expect debate and learn from it. Remember that the creation of a memorial entails the navigation of open wounds. At the United States Holocaust Memorial Museum, Director Sara Bloomfield noted, "If there is no debate, you're probably on the wrong track."

Officials at the Oklahoma City National Memorial had confronted a challenge similar to the one now facing the World Trade Center planners: how to envision a memorial so soon after the events it would memorialize. Honoring the victims of the terrorist bombing of the Alfred P. Murrah Federal Building in April 1995, that memorial opened on the fifth anniversary of the attack. Officials

Maya Lin (above) won the design contest for the Vietnam Veterans Memorial when she was just 21. The win launched her career as an architect, which has since included the Civil Rights Memorial in Alabama and Wave Field in Ann Arbor, Michigan.

had struggled to balance the same kinds of hopes as those expressed in New York, as evidenced in their mission statement: "We come here to remember those who were killed, those who survived, and those changed forever. May all who leave here know the impact of violence. May this memorial offer comfort, strength, peace, hope, and serenity."

VOICES

NATIONAL SEPTEMBER 11 MEMORIAL

Mission Statement

■ Remember and honor the thousands of innocent men, women, and children murdered by terrorists in the horrific attacks of February 26, 1993, and September 11, 2001.

■ Respect this place made sacred through tragic loss.

■ Recognize the endurance of those who survived, the courage of those who risked their lives to save others, and the compassion of all who supported us in our darkest hours.

■ *May the lives remembered, the deeds recognized, and the spirit reawakened be eternal beacons, which reaffirm respect for life, strengthen our resolve to preserve freedom, and inspire an end to hatred, ignorance, and intolerance.*

Not everyone agreed with the open competition model. In Alabama, civil rights lawyer Morris Dees, a co-founder of the organization that created the Civil Rights Memorial, told the LMDC, "The simpler, the better. Not all successful memorials are the result of competitions, committees, or drawn-out decision making." Dees had hired Maya Lin to design the memorial without a competition.

Back in New York, those who had participated in the tour attempted to distill the lessons they had learned. Some advice would continue to be a touchstone during difficult moments along the way. In the end, the most important advice shaped the path forward: to ensure ample opportunities for dialogue and conversation.

THE FAMILIES ADVISORY COUNCIL developed a draft memorial mission statement and the LMDC invited the public to give feedback about it through a mailing to over 3,000 family members of victims and a number of open hearings. Two drafting committees were then formed to digest the feedback received: one to focus on revising the mission statement, and one to develop a set of principles to guide the memorial design. The committees included victims' family members, survivors of the attacks, first responders, downtown residents, community leaders, and arts and architecture professionals. Starting with the preliminary statement developed by the Families Advisory Council, committee members weighed every word. After lengthy debates and reviews of public comments, changes included the revision of the word "killed" to "murdered" and the addition of the word "terrorists" as the perpetrators of the attacks described.

With the mission statement and a set of guiding principles in place, in April 2003, the LMDC launched what would become the largest design competition in history. Entry was open to adults 18 years of age and older, without regard to nationality or professional accreditation. All entries would be evaluated by a prestigious 13-member memorial jury that included world-renowned artists and architects, prominent arts and cultural professionals, a 9/11 victim's family member, a lower Manhattan resident and business owner, and representatives of the governor's and mayor's offices.

As competitors created their entries, the jury took part in a "Public Perspectives" campaign—a series of forums through which people could express their aspirations for the winning design. Civic and community organizations helped

Each chair in the Field of Empty Chairs (opposite) at the Oklahoma City National Memorial represents a victim of the bombing at the Alfred P. Murrah Federal Building. Nineteen chairs are smaller, in tribute to the children who were killed.

Memorial contest finalist "Lower Waters" (above), by Bradley Campbell and Matthias Neumann, used various levels of water and light to represent the emotional movement through the experience of grief and healing.

The memorial jury met with the LMDC's Families Advisory Council (right), the group of family members that had drafted the memorial mission statement, in May 2003.

Expansive fields of votive lights (above) were suspended in midair in the finalist entry "Votives in Suspension" by Norman Lee and Michael Lewis. Each votive represented a victim, its height to be determined by the victim's age.

Memorial Competition finalists Joseph Karadin with Hsin-Yi Wu envisioned two island gardens (opposite) rising from the footprints of the twin towers, supported by columns representing the victims. The entry was titled "Suspending Memory."

to conduct extensive outreach, and the LMDC partnered with over 20 victims' family organizations to send a mailing about the competition to over 6,500 households, involving as many family members as possible.

In May 2003, the LMDC held a meeting between the jury and the Families Advisory Council. The room was awash in emotion, with widely divergent views advocated passionately. Attendees debated whether the jury would have the freedom to make decisions that ran counter to policy decisions already made—including a master plan showing infrastructure in the footprints of the towers and a statement that the names of the victims would be treated without hierarchy. The Memorial Competition guidelines asked that the designs be sensitive to the spirit and vision of the master plan, but allowed that design concepts might stretch the boundaries of the guidelines if, in collaboration with the LMDC, they were deemed feasible and consistent with Libeskind's intentions.

The question of whether first responders should be recognized differently from other victims was by far the most fraught and contentious of the evening, and would remain so through the coming years.

At one emotional point, a mother recounted the pain of receiving several separate notifications about the identification of some of her son's remains and how the families of 1,400 other victims had not received any notifications at all. "We are truly not ready to think of a memorial and to think about what we need in the memorial," she said. Another talked about how difficult it was to discuss the memorial amid such heartache, saying, "Terms like 'hallowed ground' and 'sacred ground' are so much more than terms to my family, to my brother's children."

Others spoke about their loved ones' lives and the vitality that had filled them. Anthoula Katsimatides, whose brother John was killed in the north tower, said, "I think it should definitely be a place of reflection and contempla-tion. But it should also resonate with life and color . . . I want it to be a place that can make me smile. I think my brother would have wanted me to be able to pray and cry, but smile in his memory."

Tom Rogér, whose daughter Jean was a flight attendant on Flight 11, agreed, telling the jury, "My daughter wrote the night before she died a birth-day card to her boyfriend: 'May you have love, happiness, and peace of mind, because in the end everything else just comes and goes.' So that's what that memorial should show."

By taking part in this competition, you have already helped to heal our city and demonstrate, once again, New York does not stand alone.

GOVERNOR PATAKI &
MAYOR BLOOMBERG
JOINT STATEMENT, MARCH 2003
LAUNCH OF THE MEMORIAL COMPETITION

Through another public forum available by webcast, over 700 people shared their hopes and aspirations for the memo-rial design with the jury. Another meeting was held with all of the LMDC's advisory councils. All of these sessions began with a moment of silence for those killed in the attacks, followed by introductions from the jury members. Without exception, each juror at some point admitted to the daunting expanse of the job ahead. At one meeting, Susan Freedman, president of the Public Art Fund, said, "I think this is the most humbling experience of my life." Maya Lin said she hoped "to bring to the jury a sort of tension between art and archi-tecture" before confessing, "I for one am extremely scared and hope that I can do the absolute best."

One major source of tension arose between family members who wanted to ensure access to bedrock of the site, which was now widely considered "sacred ground," and downtown residents and workers who wanted the memorial to be at ground level and better integrated into the surrounding neighborhood. The master plan had called for the memorial to be kept below street level, accessed by long ramps reminiscent of those used to access ground zero during the recovery period.

Residents told stories of losing friends and neighbors, of returning to destroyed apartments after the attacks, and of the pain of circumnavigating a site of such tragedy several times a day. They reminded jurors that the World Trade Center had been a gathering place—not only where they worked, but where they lived, shopped, dined, and went to cultural events. One man, a downtown restaurant owner, talked about the diversity of the victims—regulars at his restaurant who never returned—from Cantor Fitzgerald traders to Port Authority police officers. Although he admitted he did not know what to build, he recommended that the jury "try to feel what they would want."

A downtown resident gave the last comment of the public sessions with the jury: "I certainly think the opportunity you have, and I hope it can really be realized, is to identify this as not only a healing opportunity, but to create a community where you can actually bridge all of these divisions."

MEANWHILE, AROUND THE WORLD, thousands of people were creating memorial designs. One competition participant wrote on an online blog that he was "feeling the energy of the thousands of others throughout the world focusing on this awesome project."

The breadth of response was a true testament to the global impact of the 9/11 attacks. By the deadline of June 30, 2003, 5,201 individuals and teams from 49 states and 63 countries had submitted designs for a memorial at the World Trade Center site. To be considered, applicants had to mail 30- by 40-inch presentation boards to a warehouse on West 36th Street. There, each package underwent security screening for explosives, anthrax, and other chemical agents. They were then transported to the Equitable Building near ground zero, a location that was not disclosed to the public at the time so that jurors could review the entries without interruption.

Given the unprecedented volume of submissions and thoroughness of the process, with each juror reviewing every one of the 5,201 entries, the competition took six months to complete. All told, if the competition boards were set up side by side at the same time, they would have stretched about 2.5 miles.

Finalist entry "Dual Memory" by Brian Strawn and Karla Sierralta featured glowing light portals commemorating the lives of the victims, their names and faces revealed on glass and stone.

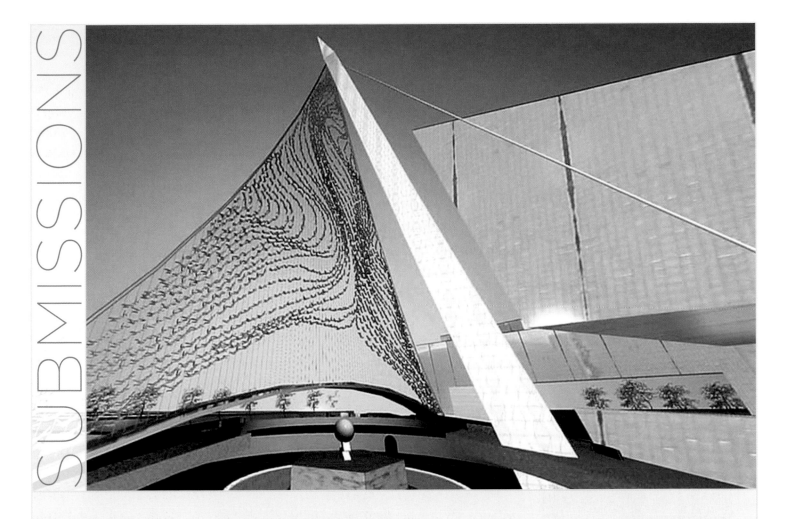

SUBMISSIONS

CONTEST ENTRIES,

including this one by Robert Jarvik, were submitted from 63 countries, among them Egypt, France, Ireland, Kuwait, Luxembourg, Russia, and South Korea.

The 5,201 entries to the Memorial Competition painted a vast array of diverse ideas, submitted by master architects and world-class artists, as well as people who had never designed a thing but were now moved to try. Entries that did not make it to the final round included one from Dr. Robert Jarvik, inventor of the Jarvik heart, who envisioned "three thousand life-size figures striving upward"—each containing a heart-shaped time capsule. An entry from Israel was a giant red heart showing "love can and must prevail." Other entries ranged from a big apple to two tremendous white planes resembling doves; from an "Endurance Chapel" to an enormous question mark to symbolize "the big questions" coming out of 9/11.

a gardener, 2 prairies, 1 orchard, one moment

"GARDEN OF LIGHTS" by Pierre David with Sean Corriel and Jessica Kmetovic, a finalist design, proposed gardens

f solitude, a new sky Garden of Lights

cultivated above two underground rooms filled with constellations of light.

Applicants were required to submit their designs on one 30- by 40-inch board (above). Strict guidelines were set; the boards had to be lightweight, unframed, and no less than ¼ inch thick, and any text had to appear in a font of at least 14 points.

The final eight designs (right) were made public on November 19, 2003, through a display in the World Financial Center, across the street from ground zero.

Vartan Gregorian, chairman of the jury, later mused that he had initially been told that the process would take "a couple of weeks."

During the first stage, the jury reviewed the submissions anonymously, using color-coded stickers to flag the entries they believed should proceed to the next round. Boards with no stickers were eliminated. Boards with only one could be kept in the competition if signaled as a "passion vote"—an entry in which a juror particularly believed. One of those eventually became one of the top three finalists. The jurors did not always agree. There were heated arguments short and long; there were deeply meaningful, soul-searching discussions. Responding to what they heard in public forums, they questioned the plan to locate the memorial at bedrock. They also came to believe that no matter what design was chosen, it must include greenery and new life. No deliberations were held without all 13 jurors present, and their notebooks remained in a double-locked office through the competition.

The selection was narrowed from 5,201 to 250; then to 25 semifinalists; and finally down to 9. One was disqualified when the jury learned its designer had submitted two entries, a guideline violation. Finally, the jury learned the identities behind the designs and met the finalists. Each individual or team received $130,000 to further develop the designs and create presentations and models.

In November 2003, the LMDC held a private screening of the eight designs for victims' families, followed by a public exhibit unveiling them to the world. Responses, professional and otherwise, spanned the spectrum. Many walked out of the exhibit in awe, mindful of the way the designs balanced respect for the victims with hope. But the designs also drew serious criticisms, marked by adjectives like "banal," "generic," and "expected." Paul Goldberger wrote in *The New Yorker* that five of the eight designs were "marred by some degree of hokeyness."

There were beautiful, touching designs by families who clearly designed these up on the kitchen table at home. There were unfortunately giant apples with planes running into them. Everything: good, bad, ugly. Our job was just to see everything.

JAMES E. YOUNG
PROFESSOR AND 9/11 MEMORIAL JUROR

"People are responding from the heart," said juror James Young, viewing the spectrum of responses as an indicator of the breadth of meaning embodied by the memorial. Whatever people thought of the finalist designs, most could not help but be moved by the outpouring of participation from six continents and across faiths, cultures, beliefs, and ethnic and racial backgrounds.

The jury continued to work with the finalists to improve their designs through the end of the year, and narrowed the field to three following intensive interviews with the designers, an array of feasibility studies, and some of the most emotional dialogues of the process. On January 5, 2004, the jurors met to make a final decision. In the morning, they heard final presentations from the teams behind the top three designs: "Memorial Cloud," "Garden of Lights," and "Reflecting Absence." The jury had established that ten votes would be required to decide the winner. The day's agenda included breakfast and lunch, and when deliberations continued, the jury stayed for dinner too.

Acutely aware of the weight of responsibility inherent in the day's decision, jury members knew the chosen design would need to speak to the families who had lost loved ones, to a city that needed a space to transcend, to people around the country and the world seeking a 9/11 memorial, and to the future.

Finalist "Inversion of Light" by Toshio Sasaki of Japan treated the two tower footprints differently. The north would contain the names of the victims and a history of 9/11. In the south, a reflecting pond would be illuminated at night.

REFLECTIONS DURING THE 2004 COMPETITION PROCESS

Paula Grant Berry, member of the LMDC Families Advisory Council whose husband, David S. Berry, was killed in the south tower of the World Trade Center: *"I was overwhelmed that so many people cared—and wanted to share our grief."*

Susan K. Freedman, president of the Public Art Fund of the City of New York: *"This is an endeavor of national, international, and historic significance."*

Vartan Gregorian, Ph.D., president of the Carnegie Corporation of New York: *"How we commemorate those who died is an historic moment when we are called upon to do justice to their memory."*

Patricia E. Harris, the deputy mayor for administration of the City of New York: *"I'm confident that the memorial design will capture the resilient spirit of New Yorkers and our determination to remain strong and hopeful in the face of seemingly unbearable challenges."*

Maya Lin, architect internationally recognized for creating the Vietnam Veterans Memorial in Washington, D.C., and the Civil Rights Memorial in Montgomery, Alabama: *"I hope that my experience with memorials can help in the process to find a powerful and moving memorial."*

Michael McKeon, managing director of Mercury Public Affairs: *"I saw firsthand the strength and courage of so many family members who lost loved ones, both in and out of uniform, on that horrible day. They lifted New Yorkers through the crisis."*

Julie Menin, president and founder of Wall Street Rising, a not-for-profit organization founded in October 2001 to help restore vibrancy and vitality in lower Manhattan: *"It must be spiritually uplifting and architecturally memorable. It must serve as an instrument of healing for the families, the city, and our nation."*

Enrique Norten, distinguished architect and educator, and co-founder of Taller de Enrique Norten Arquictectos S.C. (TEN Arquitectos): *"This memorial is about both pain and loss, but also about optimism and hope for the future."*

Martin Puryear, world-renowned artist of sculptures and major public installations: *"The panel will have the great responsibility of choosing a design which honors the victims' memory with dignity, spirit, and beauty."*

Nancy Rosen, expert consultant in public art programs and fine art collections: *"I am full of hope that this process, and its ultimate outcome, will fittingly address the tragic circumstances and sobering reality that have brought us all to this point."*

Lowery Stokes Sims, Ph.D., executive director of the Studio Museum in Harlem: *"My late father John J. Sims, Sr., worked for the Port Authority and I have fond memories of my first visit to the two towers as their construction was being completed."*

Michael Van Valkenburgh, founder and principal of Michael Van Valkenburgh Architects: *"For me, the memorial is a gift to the future."*

James E. Young, Ph.D., author, professor, and chair of the Department of Judaic and Near Eastern Studies at the University of Massachusetts, Amherst: *"If we see memory itself as a living, life-affirming process that unfolds over time, then we might come to regard this memorial as a stage in the process, not its last word."*

REFLECTIN

A **RENDERING** of the National September 11 Memorial at night reflects the final design, reached through years of

G ABSENCE

planning. More than 400 oak trees create a green roof over the belowground portions of the museum.

AN EARLY RENDERING of Michael Arad's "Reflecting Absence" design included ramps that led to the bases of the waterfalls and a narrow building for cultural programming along the site's western edge.

6

FINAL DESIGN

THE JURY DEBATED INTO THE NIGHT of January 5, 2004. Early in the day, all agreed that the "Garden of Lights" team had not addressed some of the jury's key concerns, but strong support continued for both remaining designs, "Memorial Cloud" and "Reflecting Absence." Several rounds of votes were held throughout the day, but neither design garnered the ten required votes until around 11 p.m., when 10 of the 13 jurors voted in favor of "Reflecting Absence"—a design that just days before had been described in the *New York Times* as the "dark horse" of the competition. Maya Lin, one of the design's biggest supporters from the start, noted that it "made something positive out of the void." One argument that proved convincing to jurors was that "Reflecting Absence" spoke to the site more directly than other finalists.

Your contribution will forever serve as a monument to our shared loss.

VARTAN GREGORIAN

**MEMORIAL JURY CHAIRMAN, ADDRESSING THE
5,200 MEMORIAL COMPETITORS NOT CHOSEN**

Jurors also discussed how the design would relate to the surrounding majestic spiral of office towers, and many felt that "Reflecting Absence" was the only design of a scale powerful enough to hold its own in that setting.

The selection of Michael Arad's "Reflecting Absence" was just the beginning of a long evolution in the design of the 9/11 memorial. Over the coming years of planning and construction, Arad's original vision would evolve significantly—even, in fact, before it was publicly announced as the winner.

Memorial architect Michael Arad (above) was born in London, the son of a former Israeli ambassador. He later lived in Jerusalem and served in the Israel Defense Forces before moving to the United States in 1991.

On his competition design board (opposite), Arad envisioned both "a sacred memorial ground" and "a large urban plaza that will benefit the residents of the city in their everyday lives."

MICHAEL ARAD WAS AN UNKNOWN—a 34-year-old architect for the New York City Housing Authority who had left a job designing skyscrapers at a large architecture firm to focus on projects that more directly interacted with communities, like police stations and community centers. He was the only one of the eight finalists who had entered the competition without a partner or team.

The design board Arad submitted to the competition showed a number of digressions from the master plan. Rather than retain Libeskind's suggestion that the memorial site remain within the sunken pit, he brought it back up to grade—a gesture jurors recognized as in keeping with the hopes New Yorkers had expressed that the site be knitted back into the fabric of lower Manhattan. Juror James Young later noted, "We saw pretty big problems with leaving large parts of the slurry wall depressed. It would be a big canyon, separated from the neighborhood."

Another departure from the master plan, however, was rejected by the jury during the competition process. Arad first proposed ridding the memorial quadrant entirely of any buildings, in effect discarding the notion of anything other than the memorial itself on the eight-acre block. When asked to include a museum in his design as the master plan had called for, Arad proposed a long, thin structure along the west side of the site, which he noted would also serve as a buffer between the memorial and the busy highway next to it. Such a building was deemed not to be ideally shaped to house a museum, though, so the jury asked Arad to relocate it to the northeast corner of the site, in

This design seeks to emphasize the void left by the destruction of the twin towers, a void that is both physical and emotional. The footprints of the two towers are marked by creating two square depressions thirty feet deep, in a flat field. At the bottom of each depression is a reflecting pool that is fed by a constant sheet of water that cascades down the four sides of each square pit. Each reflecting pool's surface is punctured by a square opening into which the water cascades further down, seemingly into a depthless void.

Visitors to the site can walk around each void, gazing down at the pools below them, or descend to the water level through a tunnel-like structure. Those who do, find themselves in a dark and cool space, walking down a series of stairs and ramps, the sound of water falling growing ever louder. At the bottom of their descent they emerge behind the curtain of water as it strikes the surface of the pool.

At this point the visitors find the names of the victims of the attack on the world trade center inscribed on a low stone parapet, the only element (other than the sheet of water falling from above) standing between them and the pool. As they stand there contemplating the tragedy that had occurred at this site, the sheer size of each space, and the length of the ribbon of names circling each pool, serve to physically underscore the enormity of the destruction.

After circling one of the memorial pools visitors can walk across to its twin while remaining underground, or return to the surface by a set of stairs and ramps that are similar to the ones they entered the memorial through. Their passage is marked again by darkness and a sudden return to light as the sound of water fades behind them and they emerge back upon the surface.

With respect to the master plan in the competition brief, this scheme suggests an alternative view of how the site can be integrated into the fabric of the city. It suggests continuity by remaining at street level, with a large open square that will become defined as buildings rise around it. This large open field should be punctuated only by the footprints of the two memorial pools, while other buildings that are associated with commemorating the events of September 11, such as a museum or visitor center, can be placed across the street from the open square in one of the adjacent blocks. This will allow the site to function both as a sacred memorial ground for those who descend to the memorial pools, and as a large urban plaza that will benefit the residents of the city in their everyday lives as they cross the site on their way to work or play.

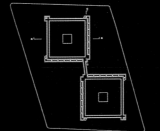

A study model built to investigate the idea of a void expressed as a tear in the surface of a sheet of water

site plan

plan at plaza level

plan at pool level

section a-a

section b-b

section c-c

accordance with the master plan. Libeskind would later agree to withdraw a proposal in his master plan for a cultural building cantilevered out over the memorial, but he would not give up the idea of culture at the corner of the site he believed would be the most active—at the intersection of two reintroduced streets running through the World Trade Center site, where the memorial would meet with cultural, commercial, and public transportation ventures.

The jury applauded Arad's minimalist approach to the two carved-out memorial pools, but they found the surrounding plaza too barren and inhospitable. When he became a finalist in the competition, they urged him to partner with an experienced landscape architect. Arad invited Peter Walker, a well-known 71-year-old California landscape architect who had also submitted a design to the competition, to join him. Walker and Arad set to work immediately, greening and softening the design with trees and landscaping.

One of the last elements to be decided before the public unveiling of the design was also one that would prove most challenging to memorial officials for years to come: the arrangement of the names of the victims. As a finalist, Arad had begun grappling with this challenge, and saw two large questions looming before him. The first was whether or not first responders should be acknowledged separately or differently from other victims—if there could be some way of marking their heroic sacrifice without diminishing the significance of the other deaths. The second was in what order the names would be arranged. Arad had the idea of "meaningful adjacencies"—a structure in which names of victims related in life could be listed together in death, one that many originally thought would be too difficult and complex to implement. Arad did not want a sense of what he called a "usual organization" like alphabetical order, especially knowing that many names were the same or similar, and that such an arrangement would actually separate families and friends. The challenge was extraordinarily emotional. "Frankly," Arad admitted, "I broke down and cried."

Arad finally settled on an arrangement that would appear haphazard, with first responders' names woven among those of the people they were trying to rescue and marked with an insignia indicating their line of work. "It was a tremendously painful decision," he said, but without his meaningful adjacencies concept, he thought it the only way to avoid unintentionally giving more value to some lost lives than others. The decision would not be final, though, and after much anguish and debate over this most personal part of the memorial,

Michael Arad and Peter Walker joined Governor Pataki, Mayor Bloomberg, and LMDC President Kevin Rampe to unveil the winning memorial design at the Federal Hall National Memorial, the site of the nation's first capitol building.

VOICES

MICHAEL ARAD AND PETER WALKER

From their Memorial Design Statement

"This memorial proposes a space that resonates with the feelings of loss and absence that were generated by the destruction of the World Trade Center and the taking of thousands of lives on September 11, 2001, and February 26, 1993. It is located in a field of trees that is interrupted by two large voids containing recessed pools. The pools and the ramps that surround them encompass the footprints of the twin towers. A cascade of water that describes the perimeter of each square feeds the pools with a continuous stream. They are large voids, open and visible reminders of the absence.

The surface of the memorial plaza is punctuated by the linear rhythms of rows of deciduous trees, forming informal clusters, clearings, and groves. This surface consists of a composition of stone pavers, plantings, and low ground cover. Through its annual cycle of rebirth, the living park extends and deepens the experience of the memorial."

SEED OF A VISION

Not long after 9/11, well before a design competition was ever announced, Michael Arad had his first idea for a memorial—quite different from the design he submitted in 2003. "I thought about a memorial actually out in the Hudson River," he said. "Two voids would be carved or cut or would break the surface of the river, and water would spill into them, and these voids would never fill up."

Arad built a model and photographed it on the roof of his apartment building, against the skyline. When the master plan was selected, he began to think about how he could adapt his concept, marking the tower footprints with waterfalls. To recall the sense of water flowing into an abyss, he added a secondary void at the center of each pool to give the sense of water flowing into them eternally without ever filling them up.

officials would return to the challenge repeatedly in the following years.

It was January 6, 2004, when the jury announced that "Reflecting Absence" was the winning memorial design. Jurors noted that significant changes had been made during the competition deliberations and would be revealed the following week. Arad and Walker used the week to further develop renderings and models, and on January 14, 2004, they unveiled their revised design at Federal Hall, near the New York Stock Exchange. Arad later described how humbled he was to present his ideas for the memorial in a building with such meaning to American history, standing with the governor, the mayor, the jurors, and most meaningfully, families of the 9/11 victims.

For the first time, the public saw the twin voids in their new green setting. The design retained the extraordinary sense of loss through negative space—but was now paired with life and resilience, a plaza that would require nurturing and care far into the future.

> ## We created a memorable and spiritual green space apart from the busy city and embracing the memorial pools.
>
> ### PETER WALKER
> **AT DECEMBER 2004 PRESS CONFERENCE RELEASING NEW MEMORIAL DESIGN DETAILS**

EVEN THOUGH THE DESIGN WAS WIDELY EMBRACED, officials knew from their experiences with the master plan that it would not be universally loved. Many family groups were pleased that "Reflecting Absence" addressed a number of their concerns—especially once they learned that additional spaces were provided at bedrock for an interpretive center, where the monumental artifacts of 9/11 would return to the World Trade Center site and be placed alongside narrative historical exhibits—a space that would ultimately become the Memorial Museum.

Others were pleased to see that the design addressed a long-fought battle over the preservation of the tower footprints. Back in 2002, Governor Pataki had stated, "We will never build where the towers stood," assuring families that the footprints would not be filled with commercial and retail spaces. Some took that commitment to mean no building anywhere on the footprints from "bedrock to infinity." The train tracks for the Port Authority Trans-Hudson (PATH)

Michael Arad partnered with Peter Walker, head of the eponymous landscape architecture firm, known for designing parks and plazas at universities and cultural institutions around the world.

The memorial (rendered here) occupies eight of the redeveloped World Trade Center site's sixteen acres. Fulton and Greenwich Streets, once part of Radio Row and later severed by the "super block" of the twin towers, will be reintroduced to separate the memorial and commercial spaces.

The Coalition of 9/11 Families printed 18- by 24-inch plastic signs (opposite) to advocate for the preservation of the twin tower footprints at bedrock. Anthony Gardner later loaned his to the 9/11 Memorial Museum.

train, however, still ran through the footprint of the south tower, 70 feet below street level at bedrock. Practical concerns had also intervened after the selection of the master plan, leading designers and engineers to propose locating substructure elements within the footprints, including truck ramps and a bus garage for eventual visitors to the site.

Learning of these complications, the Coalition of 9/11 Families, a group of leaders of several different victims' family organizations that had been started since the attacks, had launched a campaign to ensure the authentic remnants of the World Trade Center would be preserved: This included not only the slurry wall but also sections of the bedrock upon which the towers were built and the remnants of the box columns that had served as both the facades and structural supports of the towers and still remained, though sawed off during the recovery efforts. Through the coalition's dedicated efforts and the work of preservationists, the box columns are now preserved within the museum at bedrock, outlining the footprints of 1 and 2 WTC.

In response to these concerns, the LMDC worked with the Port Authority, Silverstein Properties, and the Metropolitan Transportation Authority to reconfigure the entire substructure design. To shift infrastructure off the footprints, the LMDC purchased and committed to deconstruct the former Deutsche Bank building south of the World Trade Center, which had been severely damaged on 9/11. As a result, 97 percent of the north tower footprint and 50 percent of the south tower footprint fit within the museum at bedrock. The remainder of the south footprint remained inaccessible because of the train tracks. The 2004 announcement of "Reflecting Absence" as the winning design made clear to many that the heartfelt campaign for infrastructure to be moved off the footprints had been successful.

The day after the announcement, Arad and Walker met with Daniel Libeskind to review how the memorial would fit into his master plan. The memorial was to sit at the heart of a site where some of the tallest buildings in the world were being built, along with a train station to rival Grand Central Terminal and subways and PATH trains running smack through it. The situation posed unprecedented obstacles that, inevitably, required compromises. Engineering and design challenges between the various World Trade Center projects would continue well into construction.

To realize Arad's vision in technical architectural drawings, in April 2004, the LMDC hired Davis Brody Bond (DBB) as the associate architecture firm for the memorial. Around the same time, Arad became a partner at Handel Architects, a ten-year-old firm headed by Gary Handel, whom Arad felt would be able to help him ensure his vision came to life successfully.

By December 2004, the memorial had been laid out in schematic designs, and DBB had been selected as the architect of the Memorial Museum below it. A press conference revealed new memorial details, including that over 400 oak

> I see people 500 years from now walking the footprints . . . It's that tangible connection, that direct connection to history, one that would have been destroyed had it not been for the efforts of everyday citizens convincing redevelopment officials to understand the importance of it.

ANTHONY GARDNER
DIRECTOR, SEPTEMBER 11TH
EDUCATION TRUST; FOUNDING BOARD
MEMBER, COALITION OF 9/11 FAMILIES; KEY
ADVOCATE FOR PRESERVATION ISSUES.
HIS BROTHER, HARVEY, WAS KILLED ON 9/11.

PRESERVE SACRED GROUND
FOOTPRINTS = BEDROCK TO INFINITY

INSCRIBED IN BRONZE, the names are illuminated at night through a system of lights and mirrors installed within

the parapets. Each parapet box was fabricated from a single piece of bronze that was scored and then bent into shape.

The final plan for the redeveloped World Trade Center included a spiral of five new commercial towers around the memorial, each designed by different architects (rendering, right). At 1,776 feet, 1 WTC was designed to be the tallest building in the country, as the twin towers once were.

VOICES

MEMORIAL JURY STATEMENT ON THE WINNING DESIGN

January 2004

"How to collect the disparate memories of individuals and communities together in one space, with all their various textures and meanings, and give them material form has always been the daunting challenge of any memorial site. How to commemorate at Ground Zero the countless, accumulated memories of the attacks of February 26, 1993, and September 11, 2001, tragedies shared by countless individuals and communities here and abroad, has posed an inspiring, yet humbling challenge to thousands of designers from around the world—and to us, the 13 jurors charged with finding a single memorial design only two years after the attacks . . .

Of all the designs submitted, we have found that 'Reflecting Absence' by Michael Arad, in concert with landscape architect Peter Walker, fulfills most eloquently the daunting—but absolutely necessary—demands of this memorial. In its powerful, yet simple articulation of the footprints of the Twin Towers, 'Reflecting Absence' has made the voids left by the destruction the primary symbols of our loss."

trees would be used to fill a landscaping pattern that, when viewed from one direction, seemed a randomly natural forest and, from the other, rose in stately, perfectly situated rows.

The refined design also proposed an answer to the most sensitive request that had been made by family members of those killed: the inclusion of a repository at bedrock for the unidentified remains of those killed. This initial proposal included a symbolic vessel before which visitors would be able to pay their respects, in addition to a private room for family members only and a space, to be operated by the New York City Office of Chief Medical Examiner, for the entombed remains.

The most visible change to Arad's initial design was the reduction of the number of ramps leading 30 feet belowground to the bases of the waterfalls from four to two, a change that enabled the pools to be centered exactly over the tower footprints.

> There will never be consensus in any memorial. But I think Michael Arad is truly emotionally invested in the interests of the families.
>
> **MONICA IKEN**
> **WHOSE HUSBAND, MICHAEL,**
> **WAS KILLED ON 9/11**

IN DECEMBER 2004, Governor Pataki and Mayor Bloomberg announced the launch of a private foundation to assume responsibilities for the memorial and museum from the LMDC. The organization, which would become the National September 11 Memorial & Museum, would lead fund-raising efforts and oversee the implementation of the memorial plans, while also envisioning and realizing the museum's exhibitions and operating the entire eight-acre facility in perpetuity.

Together with John Whitehead, the governor and mayor recruited a board of directors, including leading philanthropists and statesmen; banking, real estate, and media leaders; and 9/11 victims' family members who had already helped to advise the rebuilding process for years. All living former presidents of the United States also joined as honorary members. Gretchen Dykstra was named the foundation's initial president.

In addition to the memorial and museum, the master plan had allotted 250,000 square feet to two other cultural buildings—one on the site of the

Michael Arad began imagining the memorial even before the design competition was announced. An early sketch shows twin voids in the Hudson River, set partially in a cove near the World Financial Center across from ground zero.

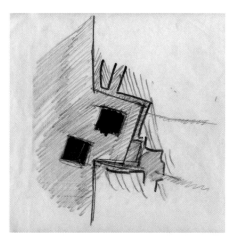

Since its inception, the National September 11 Memorial & Museum board of directors has included victims' family members and leaders from a wide range of industries, including founding directors Robert De Niro, Barbara Walters, and David Rockefeller.

memorial and a performing arts center across the street—communicating the spirit of resilience felt in the aftermath of 9/11. The LMDC chose two anchor tenants for the building on the site of the memorial and selected the Norwegian architecture firm Snøhetta, under senior partner Craig Dykers, to design it. The tenants would be a SoHo museum called the Drawing Center and a new institution called the International Freedom Center (IFC), which unexpectedly caused a passionate and widespread public debate beginning in the spring of 2005.

Planners hoped the IFC would help to fulfill the memorial mission statement's goal to "strengthen our resolve to preserve freedom, and inspire an end to hatred, ignorance, and intolerance." It would house exhibits, educational programs, and service and civic initiatives that would, IFC officials stated, "explore freedom as a constantly evolving world movement in which America has played a leading role."

A May 2005 unveiling of Snøhetta's design for the IFC building sparked protest among a group of victims' families. Led by Debra Burlingame, a 9/11 Memorial board member whose brother was the pilot of the American Airlines flight that crashed into the Pentagon, the group—which called itself "Take Back the Memorial"—argued that the IFC would politicize solemn ground. Some alleged that the IFC would somehow blame America for the attacks, which IFC officials denied, emphasizing that the institution sought to reaffirm freedom as a shining ideal to which all civilizations should aspire. The debate continued, and by the end of the summer, it had become a national and even international issue.

In the middle of the IFC tumult, the *New York Daily News* ran a piece questioning if the Drawing Center might display art inappropriate for the memorial site, causing Drawing Center leaders to recognize the restrictions that might be presented by their new home. By August, they withdrew from the site.

The next month, Governor Pataki issued a statement that the IFC could not locate on the memorial quadrant either. "There remains too much opposition," he said, "too much controversy over the programming of the IFC, and we must move forward with our first priority, the creation of an inspiring memorial." Less than an hour later, the IFC released its own statement that they were going out of business, having envisioned the center for this site and this site only.

The IFC debate confirmed once and for all that the entire eight-acre memorial site at the World Trade Center would be devoted to programming directly related to the memorial and 9/11 history. Snøhetta revised its building's design, transforming it into a smaller one initially envisioned as an orientation center

Family members of 9/11 victims organized a rally (left) at the World Trade Center site to protest the IFC and various memorial issues in the summer of 2005.

Debra Burlingame (above), whose brother, Charles—known as "Chic"—was piloting Flight 77 on 9/11, criticized the IFC in a Wall Street Journal op-ed entitled "The Great Ground Zero Heist."

When visitors first approach the site they will encounter something truly extraordinary and unexpected . . . a forest in the middle of our great city. From antiquity to today, through all of the seasons, generations of oaks have grown tall and stood strong—a reminder that, despite tragedy and loss, life endures.

STEFAN PRYOR
FIRST EMPLOYEE (2001) AND LATER
PRESIDENT (2005-2006) OF THE LOWER
MANHATTAN DEVELOPMENT CORPORATION

for visitors. Still, this was not the end of the site's evolution.

BY THE END OF 2005, with fund-raising hampered by controversies and the cost of construction escalating, many worried that momentum behind the memorial was waning. Officials grew concerned about a design that required visitors to descend belowground to see the victims' names, potentially limiting the number of visitors who could experience the most important part of the memorial. At the same time, many victims' families joined together, insisting that their loved ones' names be moved aboveground.

Governor Pataki and Mayor Bloomberg understood a new approach was needed that focused on controlling costs and expediting the project to ensure that heavy construction would begin by the fifth anniversary of the attacks. They asked Frank Sciame, a New York builder with expertise in complex cultural projects, to review the plans and make recommendations. Sciame worked closely with Michael Arad to understand his design principles and key ideas. He also worked with Max Bond, Steven Davis, and Carl Krebs from DBB, who had been grappling with hundreds of engineering challenges—including how to build an eight-acre park with 400 trees and the two largest man-made waterfalls in North America, all above active exhibition spaces at bedrock. Others included in Sciame's review were victims' family members, design and planning experts at the LMDC, and interested community voices.

All potential changes were reviewed with the 9/11 Memorial's museum director, Alice M. Greenwald, who had come from a position at the U.S. Holocaust Memorial Museum in Washington, D.C. After a month of conversations and analyses, Sciame recommended eliminating the ramps and belowground portions of the memorial and bringing the names of the victims above grade,

A photo of 9/11 victim Harvey Gardner (above) rests on one of the column remnants retained at bedrock in the museum, footprints of where the twin towers stood.

Cobblestones line most of the memorial, except in the southwest (opposite), where grass fills the Memorial Glade.

VOICES

MICHAEL ARAD
Designer of the 9/11 Memorial

" I have a sense of hope looking forward that this memorial will be successful in creating this quiet, reverent place of contemplation that allows people to gather and to find communion with each other. The site is so powerful that we need to do very little. It would be very easy to bring something to this design that would completely upset the balance of this place and focus attention on whatever we think right now is the most important thing. For me, the goal in the design has always been to remove all of the excess, to remove all of the distracting detail, and to really bring the site to its essence, to its core. "

to the top of the waterfalls. The pools and waterfalls remained as Arad had envisioned, extending nearly 200 feet along each side of the two square voids.

In another major change, the Snøhetta building at the northeast corner of the plaza became the entrance to the Memorial Museum, with a ramp leading visitors westward down to the exhibitions at bedrock. The removal of the memorial's belowground structures significantly increased the amount of museum exhibition space at bedrock within the tower footprints. Greenwald and her team of museum planners and exhibition designers—Thinc Design and Local Projects—set to work immediately, working closely with Kate D. Levin, the commissioner of the New York City Department of Cultural Affairs, to envision and realize the museum. Within the roughly acre-size north footprint would be a comprehensive exhibition covering the history of 9/11, its precursors, and the aftermath and still evolving implications. An extensive exhibit about all 2,983 individual victims was developed for the south footprint.

In response to concerns voiced by victims' family members, memorial officials removed the symbolic vessel from the design and repositioned the medical examiner's private repository for unidentified remains between the two tower footprints at bedrock, so that this sacred space would not privilege one footprint over the other. The repository would be connected to another private area for family members only. Museum designers later decided to grace the wall separating that space from the public with a simple quote from Virgil's *Aeneid,* forged in World

Trade Center steel: "No day shall erase you from the memory of time."

Overall, Michael Arad said that although the revisions included "some painful cuts to the original design," the memorial still "maintained key elements—knitting the memorial site back into the fabric of the city, and marking with two large voids the enormous absence we continue to feel."

Following on Sciame's recommendations, the Port Authority of New York and New Jersey, under its chairman, Anthony R. Coscia, and executive director, Kenneth J. Ringler, Jr., assumed responsibility for the construction management of the memorial and museum. Amanda Burden, commissioner of the NYC Department of City Planning, led a thorough review of the final design, ensuring that all details, from paving to plantings, contributed to a reverential setting.

With the project moving forward, John Whitehead informed the governor and mayor that it was time he step down as chairman of the board of the Memorial & Museum. Mayor Bloomberg volunteered to take on the job, and the board of directors voted to appoint him in October 2006. The mayor hired Joe Daniels as the president and CEO of the organization, recognizing the crucial role he had played in achieving a clear path forward while acting in that role in the months preceding. Veteran fund-raiser Cathy Blaney joined the organization to lead renewed efforts to pursue financial support for the memorial.

AT THE END OF 2006, one controversial issue that remained was perhaps the most sensitive of all: how nearly 3,000 names would be arranged on the National September 11 Memorial. In a place that would serve as a gravesite for so many who had never received remains of their loved ones—and a place that for so many others would be a journey from all corners of the world to seek an intimate connection to the tragedy they witnessed unfolding from a distance—the names would be the most personal part of the memorial experience.

> They died within that space, and it is sacred. After all this time, I have never had an opportunity to stand where my son died, where the south tower came down.
>
> **MARY FETCHET**
> FOUNDER, VOICES OF SEPTEMBER 11TH, WHOSE SON, BRAD, WAS KILLED ON 9/11, SPEAKING IN DECEMBER 2003 ON THE IMPORTANCE OF PRESERVING THE FOOTPRINTS OF THE TOWERS AT BEDROCK

In 2004, the memorial, along with other areas of the World Trade Center site, was determined eligible for listing in the National Register of Historic Places. Though a property is not normally considered for the register until 50 years have passed, when victims' families and preservationists approached the federal government, they knew the 9/11 attacks were so extraordinary and unprecedented that the site would undoubtedly be significant to American history. Dozens of interested groups participated in a consulting process to determine what must be preserved at the World Trade Center site, which led to plans to preserve and provide access to sections of the slurry wall—so integral to Daniel Libeskind's master plan concept—and the truncated box columns outlining portions of the twin towers' footprints at bedrock. In addition, the process led to the preservation of the Survivors' Staircase and other authentic remnants of the World Trade Center. All of these are visible to visitors within the museum.

The LMDC established the WTC historic preservation consulting parties in 2004 including representation from the following groups:

9/11 Widows' and Victims' Families Association
Advisory Council on Historic Preservation
Alliance for Downtown New York, Inc.
American Institute of Architects, New York Chapter
American Planning Association, New York Metro Chapter
Battery Park City Authority
Battery Park City United
Cantor Fitzgerald Relief Fund
Coalition of 9/11 Families
Coalition to Save West Street
Congressman Nadler's Office, U.S. Congress
Congresswoman Maloney's Office, U.S. Congress
Congressman Shays's Office, U.S. Congress
Delaware Nation
Families of September 11th
Governor Pataki's Office, State of New York
Greek Orthodox in America (St. Nicholas Church)

UND: BEDROCK TO INFINITY

Historic Districts Council
Hudson River Park Trust
Landmarks Preservation Commission
Lower Manhattan Cultural Council
Lower Manhattan Emergency Preservation Fund
Mayor Bloomberg's Office, City of New York
Municipal Art Society
National Trust for Historic Preservation
New York City Art Commission
New York City Community Board 1 Landmarks Committee
New York City Community Board 1 WTC Redevelopment Committee
New York City Councilmember Gerson's Office
New York City Department of City Planning
New York Landmarks Conservancy
New York State Department of Transportation
New York State Office of Parks, Recreation, and Historic Preservation
Pace University, Center for Downtown New York
Partnership for New York City
The Port Authority of New York and New Jersey
Preservation League of New York State
Rebuild Downtown Our Town
Regional Plan Association/Civic Alliance
Senator Connor's Office, New York State Senate
Senator Corzine's Office, U.S. Congress
September's Mission
Shinnecock Nation Cultural Center and Museum
Silverstein Properties
Skyscraper Safety Campaign
Speaker Silver's Office, New York State Assembly
St. Peter's Church
Tribeca Organization
Van Alen Institute
Verizon
Voices of September 11th
Wall Street Rising
WTC Families for Proper Burial, Inc.
WTC Residents Coalition
WTC Survivors' Network

MARIA PERCOCO VOLA   NOEL

DANIEL M. VAN LAERE

N NIESTADT, JR.   MARTH

HARRY BLANDIN

. IAISCHOOT

THE PARAPET DESIGN encourages visitors to touch the outlines of the names on the memorial at both day- and nighttime.

THE NAMES

As the sun sets, the names are lit from within, transforming each letter from a void in bronze to a light amid darkness.

IN EARLY ANNIVERSARY ceremonies, families laid flowers at bedrock by descending the ramp used to move material out of the site during recovery. In 2008, the ramp was dismantled to allow construction to proceed.

7

ADJACENCIES

IN THE AFTERMATH OF 9/11, people across the country and around the world began reading the names of the victims aloud at vigils—an hours-long, solemn and respectful intonation with many meanings: a prayer, a thank you for the lives shared, a tribute to their heroic acts, a struggle to comprehend how this list could ever have come to be. Beginning on the first anniversary of the attacks, New York City ceremonies for victims' families included the reading, acknowledging the importance of recognizing those taken as individuals and not statistics. Inscribed into the memorial parapets, the five rows of names stretch for more than 1,500 feet, almost a third of a mile—an expanse perhaps best described by former Mayor Giuliani, who on 9/11 called the sheer number of losses "more than any of us can bear."

The letters in each name were cut into the half-inch-thick bronze by a water jet that, at its strongest, applied 60,000 pounds of pressure per square inch.

Yet although the multiplicity of names is overwhelming, the impulse of many who approach the memorial is to trace the contours of a specific name with their fingertips, contemplating the distinctive life behind it.

NAMES ARE A CORE EXPRESSION of a person's identity, and the challenge of how to arrange the victims' names on the memorial was one of the first and most impassioned topics raised—especially given that more than 40 percent of families had not received remains of their loved ones and the site was seen as a final resting place for so many. Perhaps the most heartfelt and volatile issue woven throughout these discussions was a debate between families of uniformed personnel and those of civilians over whether or not first responders should be recognized in a unique way, distinct from other victims.

Family members and colleagues of first responders argued that their loved ones had made the ultimate sacrifice, losing their lives to save others, and that such bravery deserved special recognition. Several of them formed "Advocates for a 9/11 Fallen Heroes Memorial," calling for a separate space where all first responders would be memorialized, their names organized by agencies and units.

Families of civilians who had been killed argued that many of the victims had performed heroic acts, both in uniform and not, and that recognizing the responders differently and separately dismissed the sacrifices others made. Both sides had dozens, even hundreds of stories to tell about the brave rescue attempts on that tragic day.

Heart-wrenching discussions about what departed loved ones would have wanted dominated memorial planning meetings with families for months. In

We owe it to our future generations who visit the site, whether it is in 10 years, 50 years, a hundred years, whenever, to make sure they will immediately appreciate the magnitude of the heroes' sacrifice.

ADVOCATES FOR A 9/11 FALLEN HEROES MEMORIAL
EXCERPT FROM THE MISSION STATEMENT

Memorial architect Michael Arad envisioned that visitors would create impressions of names, a practice believed to have originated in the second century C.E., not long after the invention of paper.

If we call one of them a hero, why are we unable to do the same for all the rest? . . . In what place can we put them that will hold them above where they are now, in God's hands and where all those heroes live?

PATRICK CARTIER

FROM "WHERE HEROES LIVE," A POEM BY CARTIER, WHOSE SON, JAMES, WAS KILLED ON 9/11

April 2003, when the LMDC board voted to adopt the memorial mission statement, another resolution was appended for its consideration: "that the World Trade Center site memorial will honor the loss of life equally and the contributions of all without establishing any hierarchies."

Dozens of uniformed firefighters were in attendance. Tom Johnson, an LMDC board member who had lost his son, Scott, on 9/11, stated that he believed the best place for telling the individual stories of heroism on 9/11 would be the museum, not the memorial. On the memorial itself, he said, "any attempt to establish a hierarchy of loss is to deny the absolute measure of the tragedy visited equally on each victim and to diminish the value we put on life—all life." The resolution passed the LMDC board unanimously, but impassioned debate continued.

Michael Arad and Peter Walker's design statement, issued upon the selection of "Reflecting Absence" in January 2004, had expressed "The haphazard brutality of the attacks is reflected in the arrangement of names, and no attempt is made to impose order upon this suffering. The selfless sacrifices of rescue workers could be acknowledged with their agency's insignia next to their names." Most victims' family groups found fault with this approach, though not all for the same reasons.

For some families of first responders, the insignia was not enough. They wanted their loved ones' names listed together with their fallen colleagues, not interspersed throughout. Lee Ielpi spoke of his son, firefighter Jonathan Lee Ielpi, and his unit, Squad 288: "They came together, they went off together, and they died together." For many, beyond keeping units together, it was essential that firefighters' ranks be inscribed with their names. On the other side, for many civilian families, even the insignia recognizing first responders defied the LMDC's resolution, implying a hierarchy of importance among the victims.

Beyond the debate over how first responders should be recognized, conflict over other aspects of the order of names continued. Some wanted the names to be listed alphabetically. Others wanted to group names of victims from the

Jonathan Lee Ielpi, 29, married and the father of two boys, had started a career as a New York City police officer and later decided to follow in his dad's footsteps and become a firefighter with the FDNY. He was assigned to Squad 288 in Queens, and on the memorial he is listed alongside his buddies from Squad 288 and Hazmat 1.

same family or the same company. With the physical memorial design now defined, some suggested that only the World Trade Center victims' names be listed around the footprints of the corresponding towers they worked in, and that victims from the Pentagon and the airplanes be listed somewhere else. Firefighters and police officers continued to call for a separate structure for the names of the responders. Some wanted the names of the corporations that suffered losses on 9/11 to be engraved along with the names of their employees, while others emphatically rejected the idea, saying it would look like a corporate directory.

Hundreds of letters poured in to the LMDC about the arrangement of the names. Claire Angell Miller, for example, wrote on behalf of her brother and sister-in-law who were killed on Flight 11, David Lawrence Angell and Mary Lynn Edwards Angell: "I am asking for an exception in the case of married people who died that day . . . Lynn was David's soulmate and partner . . . It would break our hearts to see them separated, even though it is 'only' in their names." More than 60 families suffered multiple losses on 9/11. Miller's letter spoke for many.

Many of the names were arranged by hand, using slips of paper printed with each victim's name in the memorial's Optima Nova font, and noting information like affiliation and other meaningful relationships.

As Arad began meeting with families and thinking about ways to change the arrangement of names on the memorial, a number of family groups formed to try to find ways to compromise. Edie Lutnick lost her brother, Gary Frederick Lutnick, on 9/11; her other brother, Howard Lutnick, was chairman of Cantor Fitzgerald, the firm that suffered the greatest number of losses on 9/11: 658 employees. As head of the Cantor Fitzgerald Relief Fund, Edie decided to gather together families she knew disagreed with one another in an attempt to find common ground.

Ultimately, 32 representatives of various family organizations proposed a plan to list the names on the pools representing the towers in which those killed at the World Trade Center had worked, and to create headings for their companies following which the names would be listed alphabetically. Families who did not want their loved ones' names listed under a company name, or whose loved ones were visiting and not affiliated with any company, could choose to have their names inscribed on a panel of "unaffiliated" names at each pool.

The proposal suggested that Michael Arad "establish an equally significant space," separate from the two pools, for the names of those "not associated" with either tower: the first responders, the Pentagon victims, and those on the

LOVING REQUESTS

NATIONAL SEPTEMBER 11 MEMORIAL & MUSEUM
AT THE WORLD TRADE CENTER

OFFICIAL MEMORIAL NAME VERIFICATION & ARRANGEMENT FORM

I. NAME VERIFICATION (REQUIRED)

Your loved one's name appears in our records and will currently be inscribed as follows:

Scott Michael Johnson

If this listing *is correct*, please check here and proceed to Section II on the next page: ☐

If this listing *is not correct*, please request a revision within the following guidelines:

The following will be included:

- Suffixes that are name-related (e.g., Jr., Sr., III)
- Middle Names or Initials
- Hyphenated or Double Last Names
- Foreign Accents

The following will not be included:

- Prefixes or Titles (e.g., "The Honorable," "The Reverend," "Dr.," "Mr.," "Mrs.," "Ms.")
- Suffixes that are title-related (e.g., "Ph.D.," "M.D.")
- Indications of Rank
- Inscriptions in characters other than the English/Roman Alphabet

Revised name request *(please print)*: _____

The National September 11 Memorial & Museum will make every effort to ensure that your loved one's name appears as you request above. We regret that we cannot accept revisions that do not conform to the above guidelines.

Ann and Thomas Johnson   Page 1 of 5

VI. INFORMATION FOR MUSEUM EXHIBITS & MEMORIAL KIOSKS

While the following information will not appear on the Memorial, it will appear in Memorial Museum exhibits, online, and in electronic kiosks located on the Memorial Plaza.

Victim's birth date (Month / Day / Year): _____

Victim's place of birth: _____

Victim's most recent place of residence: _____

Victim's employer (note that in some cases this may be the same as the affiliation listed in Section III):

_____

Spelling of victim's name in non-Roman characters (*if applicable – e.g. Chinese, Arabic*):

_____

Victim's title/rank (if applicable): _____

WTC building where victim worked, if applicable (*e.g.*, Tower 1, Marriott): _____

WTC floor where victim worked (if applicable): _____

We invite you to please visit the "In Memory" section of our website, www.national911memorial.org, to learn about our partnership programs, including StoryCorps and the 9/11 Living Memorial, and to share additional information about your loved one to help guide the creation of exhibitions within the Memorial Museum.

If you have thoughts or suggestions regarding the Memorial names verification and arrangement process, we encourage you to contact us by e-mailing memorial@sept11mm.org or calling us toll-free at 1-877-671-1636.

VII. VERIFICATION AND CONTACT INFORMATION (REQUIRED)

Please sign here to verify that the information you have provided on this form is accurate to the best of your knowledge.

_____   _____
Signature of next-of-kin   Date

_____
Print Name

IMPORTANT: Please provide us with a phone number and email address, so we are able to contact you in the event we have questions about information you've provided on this form.

Preferred phone number: _____
Preferred email address: _____
Preferred home address: _____
_____

Ann and Thomas Johnson   Page 4 of 5

MEMORIAL STAFF *mailed verification packages to more than 3,000 addresses—the next of kin of each victim of the September 11, 2001, and February 26, 1993, attacks.*

In June 2009, the 9/11 Memorial staff sent packages of information and response forms to the next of kin of every victim. The forms asked families to verify the spelling of their loved ones' names, to verify the "grouping" and "affiliation" or company with which they had worked, and to send requests for specific names to be listed next to their loved ones' names. Memorial staff worked intensively with the NYC Office of Chief Medical Examiner, planners of the Pentagon and Flight 93 memorials, victims' family groups, and liaisons from responder agencies and corporations that had lost employees on 9/11, seeking all possible information to inform the arrangement of the names and lend the list more meaning. Over 1,200 requests were made and honored for specific names to be inscribed next to one another on the memorial.

The question of how the names are listed evokes strong feelings and convictions from relatives, colleagues, and friends of those we lost. I have spent a lot of time listening to everyone's views on the subject and there is no "right" answer. Nevertheless, it is time to move forward. I believe the solution we present today strikes the right balance and although I don't expect everyone to be happy with it, I can assure everyone that their views were heard as we struggled with this question.

MICHAEL R. BLOOMBERG
108TH MAYOR OF NEW YORK CITY
AND CHAIR OF THE 9/11 MEMORIAL BOARD

airplanes. Uniformed rescue personnel would be listed by rank and affiliation. The insignia would be removed.

Many of these ideas influenced the final names arrangement, although Arad and many others felt deeply that an entirely separate memorial for those not associated with the towers contradicted the unified spirit of the design. Others felt the idea of their loved ones being listed in an "unaffiliated" category seemed to lessen their worth and relevancy. Arad and planners continued to speak with many of the families about ways in which the essence of their proposals could be reflected in the memorial design that had been selected by the jury.

■
■

IN LATE 2006 a final compromise emerged. Arad returned to his early notion of "meaningful adjacencies," an idea that would make the arrangement of names both more complex and more personal. It would require unprecedented and dedicated outreach to the families of the victims, as well as the companies that lost employees, but the resulting placements would be powerfully infused with meaning, because the names would be arranged in accordance with geographic and familial ties, links with co-workers, and the specific wishes of the victims' loved ones.

Adopted by the board of the 9/11 Memorial in December 2006, the plan stems from the basic premise that the names would be organized by nine groups broadly defined by the locations and circumstances in which victims found themselves during the attacks. Around the north pool: those working in or visiting the north tower; those aboard Flight 11, which crashed into that tower; and the victims of the 1993 bombing, which occurred in the subbasement below it. Around the south pool: those working in or visiting the south tower; those

aboard Flight 175, which crashed into that tower; the Pentagon victims; Flight 77 victims; those in the vicinity of the World Trade Center; and the first responders.

Other ways to bring meaning flow from that basic premise. Within each grouping, the names of colleagues are together, such as the 73 employees of Windows on the World or the 35 people who worked for Fred Alger Management, or the crews of each of the four flights. First responders' names are organized by headings indicating their agencies and units—a special distinction, but a part of the unified memorial.

The deepest and most personal meaning was created by the next of kin of the victims themselves, who were offered the opportunity to ask that specific names be inscribed alongside those of their loved ones. These requests ultimately defined the entire arrangement and allowed the names of those who knew one

On the memorial, the names run continuously for hundreds of feet. Michael Arad's team and memorial staff found printed scrolls the best way to review large sections of the arrangement at once.

A screenshot from computer software (above) developed to help arrange the names shows a working draft of the entire north pool arrangement. The names of victims from Cantor Fitzgerald, the brokerage firm that lost 658 employees, are shown in various colors, representing the different departments in which they worked.

another in life—whether spouses, fiancés, siblings, co-workers, best friends, or in some cases entire families—to reside on the memorial together in death.

Though many families were pleased with the new arrangement, some controversies remained, including many firefighters' ongoing requests that ranks be included for first responders. Arad and other officials struggled with these requests. Staff had sought advice from people involved in memorials across the country, including the Vietnam Veterans Memorial, the International Association of Fire Fighters' memorial to the fallen, and the National Law Enforcement Officers Memorial, each of which had decided to list names without ranks, showing the fallen as equals side by side. Officials believed, however, that creating a distinct section of the memorial titled "First Responders," along with separate headings within that defined the agencies and units of those listed, was an important recognition of the distinct and heroic role that first responders had played on 9/11.

The staff of the memorial began conducting an enormously complex process to come up with the optimal arrangement of names, working with families and companies that lost employees to gather information about those who were killed and ensure that thousands of intricate and heartfelt relationships would be honored.

Fortified with a new depth of knowledge about each victim, including over 1,200 "adjacency requests" made by victims' families, memorial staff compiled information for Arad and his team to begin actually arranging the names and ensuring that those who knew and loved one another could be listed side by side. Memorial staff also provided sets of complex illustrations showing requests made by victims' families, and a computer program designed by the media firm Local Projects that ran an algorithm to find the best ways to meet them. Through these methods and a careful, painstaking process through which each name was placed by hand, Arad and his staff gave each of the 2,983 names its permanent space.

The process to come to the final arrangement of names, with its extraordinary level of personal meaning reflective of so many intimate relationships, was unprecedented by any memorial anywhere in the world.

> What is most gratifying to me is that I can imagine friends and family members who lost loved ones coming to the site and seeing names they know next to one another, and I hope taking some solace in that moment of tribute.
>
> **MICHAEL ARAD**
> DESIGNER OF THE 9/11 MEMORIAL

LITERALLY THOUSANDS OF STORIES lie behind why each name appears where it does. It would be impossible to convey fully in these pages the depth and intricacies of the relationships among them; instead, here are a few selected examples that instill the National September 11 Memorial with profound and personal meaning.

THE WORLD TRADE CENTER: Victims' names representing the different corporations and affiliations of the north and south towers are grouped together under the two "World Trade Center" headings: one on the north and the other on the south memorial pool. One company—the international brokerage firm Cantor Fitzgerald—experienced a loss so severe that its employees make up nearly a quarter of the names on the entire memorial. The firm operated out

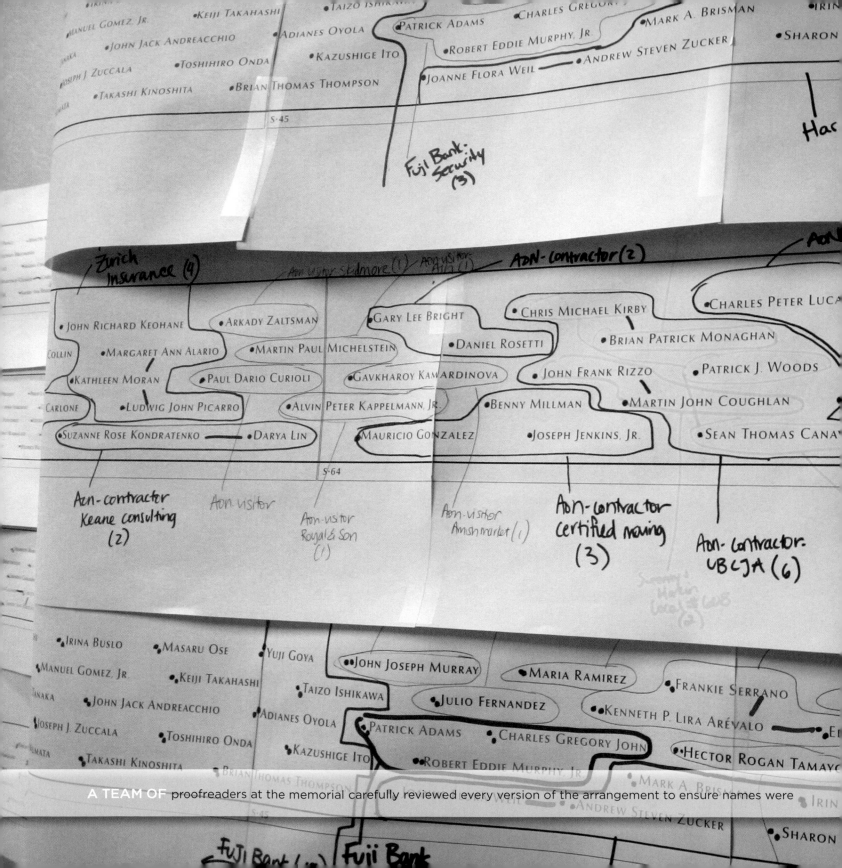

A TEAM OF proofreaders at the memorial carefully reviewed every version of the arrangement to ensure names were

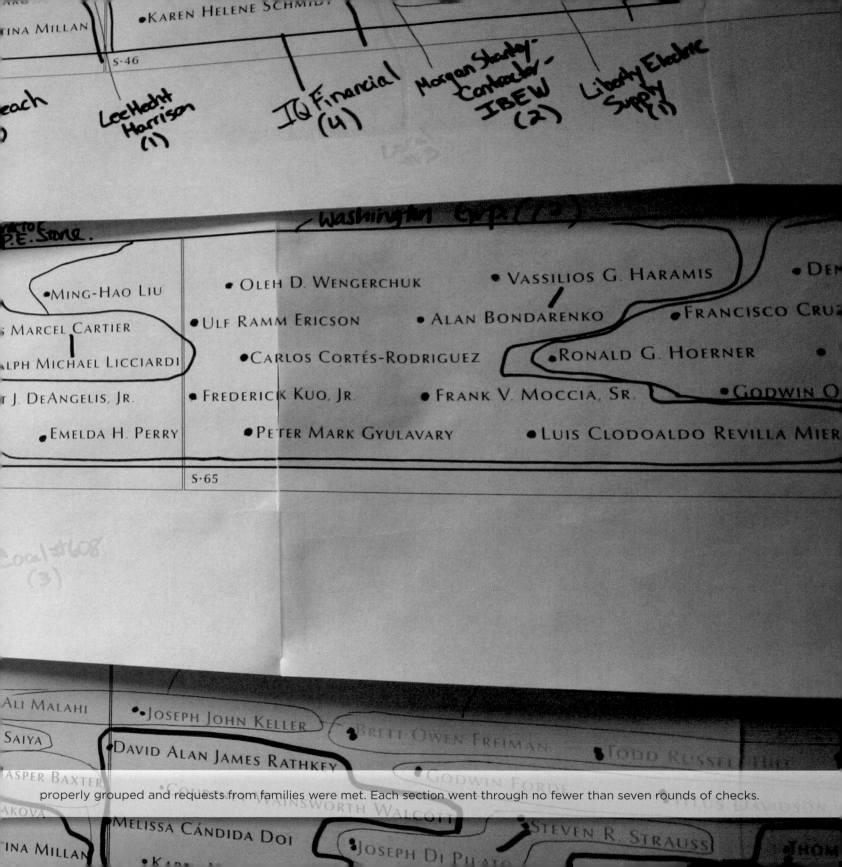

KAREN HELENE SCHMIDT

...INA MILLAN

S·46

...each

LeeHecht Harrison (1)

IQ Financial (4)

Morgan Stanley- Contractor- IBEW (2)

Liberty Electric Supply (1)

Washington Grp. (13)

...ctor P.E. Stone.

•MING-HAO LIU

•OLEH D. WENGERCHUK

•VASSILIOS G. HARAMIS

•DEN...

...MARCEL CARTIER

•ULF RAMM ERICSON

•ALAN BONDARENKO

•FRANCISCO CRUZ

...LPH MICHAEL LICCIARDI

•CARLOS CORTÉS-RODRIGUEZ

•RONALD G. HOERNER

...J. DEANGELIS, JR.

•FREDERICK KUO, JR.

•FRANK V. MOCCIA, SR.

•GODWIN O...

•EMELDA H. PERRY

•PETER MARK GYULAVARY

•LUIS CLODOALDO REVILLA MIER...

S·65

Local #608 (3)

ALI MALAHI

•JOSEPH JOHN KELLER

BRETT OWEN FREIMAN

•TODD RUSSELL HIGH...

...SAIYA

•DAVID ALAN JAMES RATHKEY

...ASPER BAXTER

GODWIN FORDE

...WAINSWORTH WALCOTT

...AKOVA

MELISSA CÁNDIDA DOI

•STEVEN R. STRAUSS

...INA MILLAN

JOSEPH DI PILATO

THOM...

properly grouped and requests from families were met. Each section went through no fewer than seven rounds of checks.

of the 101st to 105th floors of the north tower of the World Trade Center. Flight 11 hit the building at the 93rd floor at 8:46 a.m., and everyone in the Cantor Fitzgerald offices by that time was killed: 658 employees out of the roughly 1,000 who worked in New York, along with 46 contractors, food service workers, and visitors. Of the husbands who were killed, 38 of them left behind pregnant wives. There were wedding plans in the making for 46 others. When the 658 Cantor lives were taken, 955 sons and daughters lost a father or a mother.

VOICES

HOWARD LUTNICK

Chairman of Cantor Fitzgerald, who survived 9/11 only because he arrived at work an hour late, having taken his son, Kyle, to his first day at school

"My firm had the top floors of the World Trade Center. All of my friends, all of my employees, my brother, everybody was in the building working because we're a Wall Street financial services firm and at 8:46 in the morning the show is on, it's been on for an hour, and everybody's going to be there, it's not a vacation day, it's just September 11th, a day when everybody's at work.

When I got there I stood at the door and started grabbing people coming out, asking them what floor they were coming from. Sixty, 71, 82, and the highest floor I got to was 92. Then I heard this noise. It was sort of like the combination of a jet engine and this roaring breaking steel, a sound I had, of course, never heard before … So here the building is coming down behind me, it's coming at me from the side, I'm done, I dive under a car, I put my head next to the tire figuring if something crushes the car maybe the tire will bounce, but I wasn't savvy enough even to cover my mouth with a cloth or my clothes or anything, I'm just laying there … The world goes black and I'm laying there holding my breath, hold your breath, hold your breath, hold your breath. It was dead silent.

And I knew—I knew right then, I knew in my soul that they had all died, that anyone who was still in that building was gone. There was no way out for them. Six hundred and fifty-eight people. My brother Gary, my best friend Doug, 200 people who I personally hired, great people. We had a rule at the firm that we should hire our friends, that life's too short, we wanted to work with people we liked. And that rule not only applied to me where I hired my best friend and my brother, but it also applied to the guys who were the security guards who worked with their brother and their brother-in-law. We lost them all that day. Unthinkable. Impossible. "

On a list of families that sustained multiple losses on 9/11, by far the affiliation most repeated is Cantor Fitzgerald, owing partly to the family-oriented nature of the firm's culture. Unlike many other corporations, Cantor encouraged its employees to hire family members and lifelong friends. The meaningful adjacencies concept allowed these relationships to be part of the names arrangement.

Edie Lutnick, the head of the Cantor Fitzgerald Relief Fund, worked diligently for months on an emotional process to ensure that the arrangement of the Cantor victims' names would be as meaningful as possible, laying out arrangements of those who shared workspaces, who had lunch together, who went to the same colleges, who were godparents to one another's children.

Around both the north and south memorial pools, the entire structure of the arrangement—from the order of the major geographic groupings to which company would follow the one before it—was driven by the personal adjacency requests from victims' families. The World Trade Center grouping on the north pool, for example, immediately follows Flight 11 and begins with the names of

> It is heartbreaking and beautiful to think of them together that way, and it will be so special to be able to reflect on them so closely.
>
> **ABIGAIL ROSS GOODMAN**
> WHOSE FATHER AND BEST FRIEND DIED
> ON 9/11; THEIR NAMES APPEAR
> NEXT TO ONE ANOTHER ON THE MEMORIAL

Architecturally, raised words marking the start of a group like "WORLD TRADE CENTER" are composed of "prismatic" letters. Each was formed and outlined by machine before hours of finishing, completed by hand.

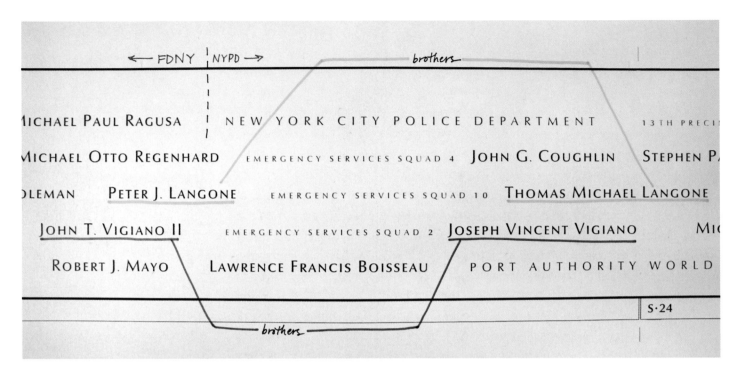

← FDNY ┊ NYPD → brothers

MICHAEL PAUL RAGUSA ┊ NEW YORK CITY POLICE DEPARTMENT 13TH PRECI

MICHAEL OTTO REGENHARD EMERGENCY SERVICES SQUAD 4 JOHN G. COUGHLIN STEPHEN P.

OLEMAN PETER J. LANGONE EMERGENCY SERVICES SQUAD 10 THOMAS MICHAEL LANGONE

JOHN T. VIGIANO II EMERGENCY SERVICES SQUAD 2 JOSEPH VINCENT VIGIANO MIC

ROBERT J. MAYO LAWRENCE FRANCIS BOISSEAU PORT AUTHORITY WORLD

S·24

brothers

Stacey Leigh Sanders, left, was 25 on 9/11. On the memorial, her name appears next to the name of her best friend's father, Richard Barry Ross, right, who died aboard Flight 11.

the 293 people who worked for Marsh and McLennan Companies, an insurance brokerage and risk consulting firm, because of a request that the names Richard Barry Ross and Stacey Leigh Sanders be listed together. Richard was a passenger on Flight 11. His oldest daughter, Abigail, lost not only her father but also her best friend, Stacey, who was at work at her new job at Marsh on the 96th floor of the north tower when Flight 11 crashed into it. The request is a poignant example of how the names arrangement allowed meaning not only among the victims, but also for the loved ones left behind.

Similarly, a personal request connected the first responders section of the memorial with the beginning of the World Trade Center section on the south memorial pool. Donald James McIntyre, a Port Authority police officer for 15 years, had been on duty on February 26, 1993, helping escort workers to safety during the first attack on the World Trade Center. On 9/11, he and his wife's cousin, John Anthony Sherry, were both there. John was a trader at Euro Brokers in the south tower. When Donald called his wife that morning, he told her he was rushing to the 84th floor, where John's offices were located. For their names to be next to one another along the south pool, the World Trade Center section on the south memorial pool immediately follows the First Responders

section and the 37 Port Authority Police Department names, with the 61 Euro Brokers names listed first. Most of the requests for personal adjacencies within the World Trade Center groupings occurred within a single affiliation, whether a family member visiting another—like Christine Egan, who was visiting her brother Michael Egan at Aon—or simply co-workers who worked side by side for weeks, years, or decades.

Some of the adjacency requests were more unusual, though—between people who barely knew one another but who formed intense bonds during that chaotic September morning, as reported by their loved ones. One such pair is Victor Wald, a stockbroker and only victim from Avalon Partners, and Harry Ramos, the head trader and only victim from May Davis Group. During the attacks, Victor tried descending the staircase but found it harder and harder to keep going. Somewhere around the 55th floor of the south tower, he decided to stop and wait for help. Many people passed by until Harry stopped. "I'm not going to leave you," he was overheard saying to the stranger. According to several survivors, Harry helped Victor down the stairs until he could go no farther. On the form Victor's wife returned to the memorial staff, she requested his name appear next to Harry's because he "died alongside of him."

FIRST RESPONDERS: For purposes of the memorial, a first responder is defined as a recipient of the 9/11 Heroes Medal of Valor awarded by President George W. Bush on September 9, 2005. Recipients included the members of the Fire Department of New York, New York Police Department, and Port Authority Police Department, as well as emergency medical services workers and others.

Unlike other sections of the memorial, the first responders' names follow headings indicating their agencies and units, listed in horizontal rows following their unit titles, such as Ladder 10. Vertically, above and below each unit, appear others that shared the same firehouses and precincts. The layout further incorporates an intricate web of requests from families who sustained multiple losses or who knew their loved ones would want to be listed with lifelong friends. All such requests were honored, over 50 within the FDNY section alone.

A number of adjacency requests crossed between two responder agencies, notably between the FDNY and NYPD. The Langone brothers, Peter with

The Vigiano brothers (above, top) followed in family footsteps when they became first responders. John received the same badge number as his grandfather: 3436. On 9/11, Joe was 34 years old and John was 36. Victims Peter and Thomas Langone (above, bottom) were brothers, both married with two children. On the memorial, the names of both pairs of brothers appear side by side (opposite, top), even though they served in different first responder organizations.

pilot

husband and wife, both flight crew

FLIGHT 77   DAVID M. CHARLEBOIS   TODD H. REUBEN   MARI-RAE SOPPER   J. JOSEPH FERGUSO

CHARLES F. BURLINGAME III   JENNIFER LEWIS   GEORGE W. SIMMONS   DIANE M. SIMMONS   DORA MAR

MARY JANE BOOTH   KENNETH E. LEWIS   NORMA LANG STEUERLE   ROBERT PENNINGER   YENENEH BETR

MICHELE M. HEIDENBERGER   SANDRA DAWN TEAGUE   LESLIE A. WHITTINGTON   CHARLES S. FALKENBERG

RENÉE A. MAY AND HER UNBORN CHILD   YVONNE E. KENNEDY   DANA FALKENBERG   ZOE FALKENBERG   CHANDL

S·69

family (husband and wife, two daughters)

FDNY Squad 252 and Thomas with NYPD Emergency Service Squad 10, both responded to the 1993 bombing and were killed responding to the 9/11 attacks. "Tommy and Peter Langone grew up in a world where dealing with danger was a family tradition," a loved one posted on a Squad 252 memorial website. "They were both following their essential dream; they were trying to save lives."

Likewise, John and Joseph Vigiano were brothers who responded with the FDNY and NYPD, respectively. "Two of the tightest brothers you could ever find," read their *New York Times* "Portrait of Grief."

THE FLIGHTS: Following the headings for Flights 11, 175, 77, and 93, the names of the crew members appear first, followed by the passengers. Some of the most heartrending stories of families experiencing multiple losses come from these flights.

On Flight 77 was a family of four: Charles S. Falkenberg and Leslie A. Whittington, who had been married for 17 years, and their children Zoe and Dana, eight and three years old. The flight to Los Angeles was intended to be just the start of the family's trip to Australia, where Leslie was to work as a visiting professor. They had been planning the trip excitedly with their daughters for

Husband and wife Charles Falkenberg and Leslie Whittington, with their two young daughters, took Flight 77 as the first leg of a journey to Australia. Their names appear together on the memorial poster (above).

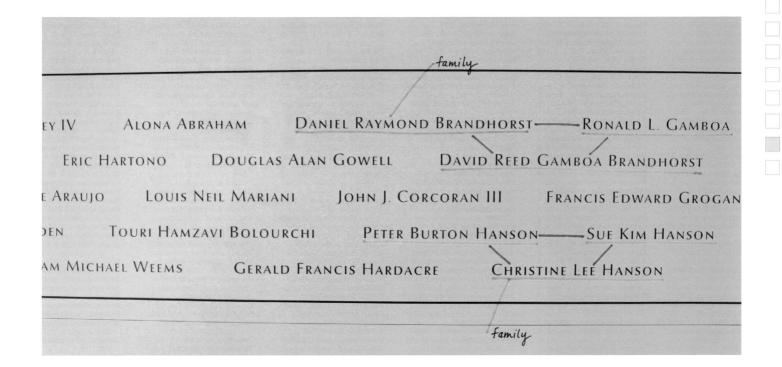

family

EY IV   ALONA ABRAHAM   DANIEL RAYMOND BRANDHORST———RONALD L. GAMBOA

ERIC HARTONO   DOUGLAS ALAN GOWELL   DAVID REED GAMBOA BRANDHORST

E ARAUJO   LOUIS NEIL MARIANI   JOHN J. CORCORAN III   FRANCIS EDWARD GROGAN

DEN   TOURI HAMZAVI BOLOURCHI   PETER BURTON HANSON———SUE KIM HANSON

AM MICHAEL WEEMS   GERALD FRANCIS HARDACRE   CHRISTINE LEE HANSON

family

months. The memorial arrangement places the names of the parents directly above their children's.

On Flight 175, a family of three: Daniel Raymond Brandhorst and Ronald L. Gamboa, who were traveling with their son, David Reed Gamboa Brandhorst, also only three years old. Like members of the Falkenberg/Whittington family, these three are among the many examples of families who would have been separated in an alphabetical arrangement of names.

On the same bronze panel appear the names of the Hanson family—Sue and Peter with their daughter Christine, at two and a half years old, the youngest victim of the 9/11 attacks. The family was on the way to visit Sue's family in Korea, flying through Los Angeles. Peter had called his father from the plane at 8:52 a.m. to tell him he thought they had been hijacked and to ask him to call United Airlines. He called again at 9:00. That call ended abruptly; his father turned on the television and saw Flight 175 hit the south tower.

Among the names of those aboard Flight 93 is Todd M. Beamer, one of the passengers who fought the terrorists and became such an inspiration in the days to follow. Using a phone from the back of a plane seat, he contacted an operator named Lisa Jefferson, reporting to her that the plane had been

The Hanson family—Peter, Sue, and their daughter Christine—was aboard United Airlines Flight 175. When entire families appear on the memorial, the names of parents are placed side by side, immediately above the names of their children.

MEMORIAL KEY

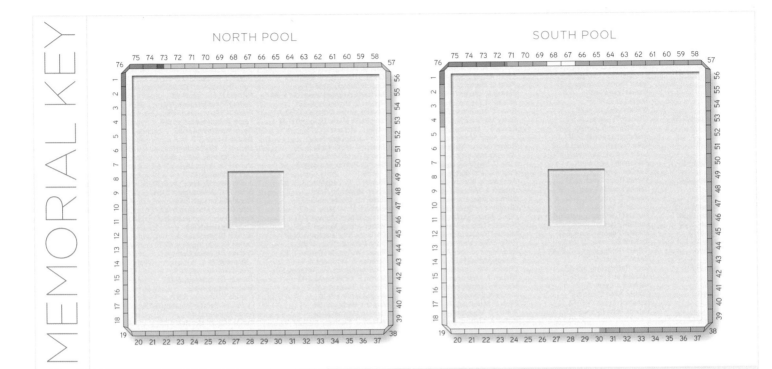

NORTH POOL

SOUTH POOL

The 2,983 names of the men, women, and children killed in the attacks of September 11, 2001, and February 26, 1993, are inscribed into bronze parapets surrounding the twin memorial pools, located in the footprints of the twin towers. Around the north pool appear the names of: those who worked in or were visiting 1 World Trade Center on 9/11; the crew and passengers of American Airlines Flight 11; and those who were killed in the February 26, 1993, bombing of the World Trade Center. Around the south pool appear the names of: those who worked in or were visiting 2 World Trade Center or other areas of the WTC complex on 9/11; the first responders; the crew and passengers of United Airlines Flight 175, American Airlines Flight 77, and United Airlines Flight 93; and those who worked in or were visiting the Pentagon.

Following each of these headings, the names are arranged so that those belonging to the same affiliation are listed together. Relatives of victims then made more than 1,200 requests for specific names to be listed alongside their loved ones, ensuring names would be inscribed alongside relatives, friends, and colleagues.

hijacked, and that he and several other passengers had a plan. In the course of the conversation, Jefferson prayed the Lord's Prayer with Beamer, and she later recalled the last words she heard from him: "Are you ready? Okay. Let's roll!"

In the Flight 77 section appear the names of a group of teachers and schoolchildren whose loved ones requested they be listed together. Three 11-year-old students—Bernard C. Brown II, Asia S. Cottom, and Rodney Dickens—were en route to the Channel Islands off the coast of Santa Barbara, California, for a four-day National Geographic Society school trip, chaperoned by their teachers and two National Geographic Society staff members.

Stories of multiple losses within one family are not limited to the passengers. Jennifer and Kenneth E. Lewis, flight attendants on Flight 77, which crashed into the Pentagon, were husband and wife, referred to by friends and colleagues as "Kennifer." They are listed on the same panel as Capt. Charles "Chic" Burlingame, who was piloting Flight 77. One of the artifacts discovered in the debris at the Pentagon was a laminated prayer card he was carrying. One side notes the scripture "Blessed are those who mourn" and the other is printed with a poem entitled "I Did Not Die."

Other crew whose names are listed side by side worked together to respond to the terror-filled skies—including flight attendant Betty Ann Ong and her crewmates on Flight 11, whose phone conversations with airline services on the ground showed incredible poise and professionalism under the direst circumstances.

As in the other flight sections, the names of the United Airlines Flight 175 flight attendants are inscribed together. They thought of one another as family, and after 9/11, several fellow flight attendants used retired airline uniforms to create memorial quilts for the families of their lost colleagues, and another featuring all their names for the 9/11 Memorial Museum.

THE PENTAGON: The Pentagon section of the memorial lists the 125 names of those who were killed in the building when Flight 77 crashed into it. As with other sections of the memorial, the names of those within the same affiliation are listed together, including members of the Army, Navy, and civilians working for military branches. The family of Angela M. Houtz, a 27-year-old Navy professional and the first civilian ever to hold her post at the Pentagon,

Daniel Brandhorst (pictured above) and Ronald Gamboa adopted their son David in 1998. The family was aboard Flight 175, traveling home to Los Angeles from vacation.

Ann C. Judge and J. Joseph Ferguson (above) were National Geographic Society employees traveling with teachers and schoolchildren on a trip to the Channel Islands.

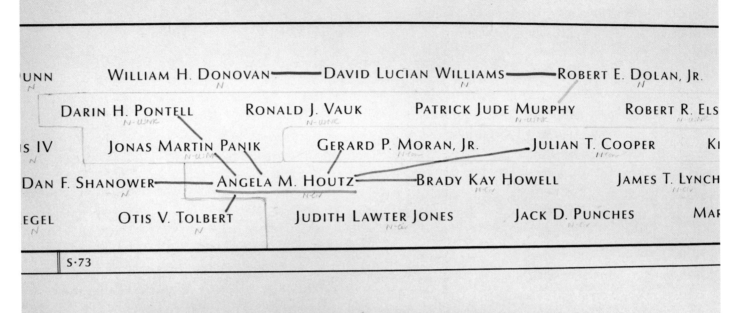

UNN   WILLIAM H. DONOVAN———— DAVID LUCIAN WILLIAMS————ROBERT E. DOLAN, JR.

DARIN H. PONTELL   RONALD J. VAUK   PATRICK JUDE MURPHY   ROBERT R. ELS

IS IV   JONAS MARTIN PANIK   GERARD P. MORAN, JR.   JULIAN T. COOPER   KI

DAN F. SHANOWER———— ANGELA M. HOUTZ————BRADY KAY HOWELL   JAMES T. LYNCH

EGEL   OTIS V. TOLBERT   JUDITH LAWTER JONES   JACK D. PUNCHES   MAF

S·73

Angela M. Houtz, who went by Angie, was killed in a conference room at the Pentagon. Her name is surrounded by the names of those who were with her in the room.

Only a small fragment of rose-colored granite from the memorial to the 1993 bombing victims (opposite) survived on 9/11, and is displayed in the 9/11 Memorial Museum.

requested seven different personal adjacencies, all now listed around Houtz's name on the memorial.

"When Angie died, she was in a conference room with her co-workers, responding to the attacks in New York, when the plane hit," her mother, Julie Shontere, explained. She wanted her daughter's name placed among the names of those who had shared their final moments together.

FEBRUARY 26, 1993: Because the bomb that had been left in a van on February 26, 1993, exploded under the World Trade Center's north tower, the six names of the victims of that attack are listed on the north memorial pool. From 1995 to 2001, a memorial fountain to these six, designed by Elyn Zimmerman, had stood on the plaza of the World Trade Center. Though it was destroyed on 9/11, a fragment bearing the name "John" was found in the rubble. "John" refers to John DiGiovanni, a dental equipment salesman who was in the parking garage on the way to a meeting when the bomb exploded. Now his name appears alongside that of Wilfred Mercado, an employee of the Windows on the World restaurant who was checking food deliveries in the basement that day.

Alongside these two names are those of the four other 1993 bombing victims, all of whom worked for the Port Authority of New York and New Jersey. Three were mechanical supervisors—Robert Kirkpatrick, Stephen A. Knapp, and William Macko—and one, Monica Rodriguez Smith, was a secretary. Monica, 35 years old, was an expectant mother when she was killed, and on the 1993 memorial, her name had been followed by the words "and her unborn child."

Adhering to this precedent, the forms sent to the next of kin of all 9/11 victims included the option of indicating that a loved one was pregnant at the time of her death. In total, there are 11 instances of families who requested that their loved ones' names be inscribed with the words "and her unborn child" on the 9/11 Memorial.

THESE FEW EXAMPLES stand for the many stories and requests that drove the arrangement of names on the memorial parapets. Again and again, the requests from loved ones of those who were killed informed the design in which the names are inscribed.

The challenge of designing the physical structure that would display the names with the necessary respect and solemnity proved to be one of the most difficult for the team of memorial designers and architects. They worked through many months and created options A through Y, almost running out of letters of the alphabet before coming to a final decision. Through all the design discussions, one common theme arose: the importance of allowing a direct, natural, and tactile relationship between the visitor, the names, and the water.

Sketches, drawings, and miniature mock-ups of panels in glass, wood, steel, and bronze were studied, refined, and discarded. Several of the more

We learned we would have a boy, and named our son Eddie. Nobody could ever have prepared me for the feelings I was experiencing. I had lost my wife, my best friend, my idol, and my son. I would never get the chance to tell Monica how much I loved her. I would never get to tell her what an inspiration she had been . . . We would never get to hear Eddie say his first word, to say "mommy," "daddy," "love."

ED SMITH
WHOSE WIFE, MONICA RODRIGUEZ SMITH, WAS EXPECTING WHEN SHE WAS KILLED IN THE 1993 WORLD TRADE CENTER BOMBING

IN MEMORIAM

This exhibition honors the 2,977 individuals killed as a result of the terrorist acts of September 11, 2001 at this site as well as at the Pentagon and in Somerset County, Pennsylvania, and the six individuals killed in the terrorist bombing of the World Trade Center on February 26, 1993.

STACEY LEIGH SANDERS

faces and names surrounds an inner chamber, where individual profiles, photos, and audio remembrances are featured.

promising designs were mocked up as full-scale sections at the Brooklyn Navy Yard, in an abandoned field large enough to represent the full expanse of the memorial pools.

In some designs, the names were inscribed at ground level, creating a striking experience of the waterfalls but taking the focus too far off the names. The final design places the names waist-high, tilted slightly so that a visitor can touch every row. In this design, the names truly became the memorial, as had been envisioned by so many from the beginning. Visitors bow their heads to read the names in a natural gesture of reverence.

Perhaps the most often expressed desire was for a fitting sense of permanence—a gravitas and material that would last, ensuring that hundreds of years from now, the names of the men, women, and children killed on

After a name parapet mock-up was created at the Brooklyn Navy Yard, a waterfall mock-up was also installed at to-scale distance to give designers a sense of how the falling water and bronze panels would interact outdoors.

September 11, 2001, would remain. Responding to this idea, Arad's design includes stone footings creating a basin or water table flowing away from the visitor eight feet horizontally before reaching the springing point for the waterfalls. The bronze parapets into which the names are cut top these stone basins, giving the appearance that, despite their heavy permanence, they are somehow floating above the water.

Visitors approaching the memorial can see the names for some distance. To ensure that all visitors, including children and people in wheelchairs, can see over the parapets and into the center void of the pools, Arad decided to chamfer the corners of the squares—cutting them diagonally, just as the corners of the twin towers had been.

Memorial designers also explored the interaction of names and water: whether water should trickle over the names themselves, creating a veil of tears, or whether names should break through a water surface like thousands of miniature islands.

In the realized design, headings and subheadings on the memorial—like "World Trade Center," "The Pentagon," or "Flight 11"—are forged in raised letters atop the bronze panels, while the names of the victims are cut through, themselves becoming reflections of absence. The water flows beneath the bronze panels, but the panels remain dry so that visitors can make rubbings or impressions of the incised names with paper and pencil, as they do at the Vietnam Veterans Memorial. At night, light shines up through the voids left by each letter, filling the absence.

As the buildings rise around the memorial, the 2,983 names are there in quiet witness. Cut through bronze, absences filled with light in times of darkness, they remind us of those who were taken from the world too soon.

> The edge of the voids is the most highly charged space in the memorial. It is a physically and symbolically important place. It is up to the edge that we lead visitors to reflect on the events of the day and the lives that were lost. It is here that they are confronted with the names of thousands who perished that day, and it is here that the scale of the towers is made clear.
>
> **MICHAEL ARAD**
> **DESIGNER OF THE 9/11 MEMORIAL**

"Now come the names, the list of casualties we are only beginning to read: They are the names of men and women who began their day at a desk or in an airport, busy with life. They are the names of people who faced death and in their last moments called home to say, be brave and I love you. They are the names of passengers who defied their murderers and prevented the murder of others on the ground. They are the names of men and women who wore the uniform of the United States and died at their posts. They are the names of rescuers—the ones whom death found running up the stairs and into the fires to help others. We will read all these names. We will linger over them and learn their stories, and many Americans will weep."
—**President George W. Bush,** Remarks at the National Day of Prayer and Remembrance, delivered September 14, 2001

"When I hear the names of those lost, they remind me of my neighbors and classmates from my childhood. I pray for the survivors and for their families. May God hold them close."
—**Sheila H.,** "Note of Hope" left at a memorial steel beam signing in Fort Wayne, Indiana

"We started going to memorial services, and it was hard to keep track of when and who and where. There were so many. I couldn't handle it all. I died that day too. Who I was, who I wanted to be. It all left that day, it all changed. The enormity of that day can disguise the individuals who were lost, but they were my friends."
—**Monica O'Leary,** who lost hundreds of her Cantor Fitzgerald friends and colleagues on 9/11

"I believe that when you lose a loved one you gain an angel whose name you know."
—**Oprah Winfrey,** hosting the "Prayer for America" service at Yankee Stadium, September 23, 2001

"I will tell my children that they should always remember what happened, and they should always remember the names of the people who died."
—**Davonte B.,** "Note of Hope" left at a memorial steel beam signing in Columbia, South Carolina

"Please remember these were real people with families and friends. They were not a number, a fact, or a statistic. These victims and heroes all had names and lives."
—**Annette M.,** "Note of Hope" left at a memorial steel beam signing in Cincinnati, Ohio

"We gather here, at the Pentagon, where the names of the lost are forever etched in stone. We gather in a gentle Pennsylvania field, where a plane went down and a 'tower of voices' will rise and echo through the ages. And we gather where the Twin Towers fell, a site where the work goes on so that next year, on the 10th anniversary, the waters will flow in steady tribute to the nearly 3,000 innocent lives. On this day, it's perhaps natural to focus on the images of that awful morning—images that are seared into our souls. It's tempting to dwell on the final moments of the loved ones whose lives were taken so cruelly. Yet these memorials, and your presence today, remind us to remember the fullness of their time on Earth."
—**President Barack Obama,** Remarks at the Pentagon Memorial on September 11, 2010

"So many names, there is barely room on the walls of the heart."
—from "The Names"
by U.S. Poet Laureate **Billy Collins**

BUILDING TH

E MEMORIAL

The occasion made the front page of a local New York newspaper and quickly circulated among national news sources.

THE MEMORIAL PLAZA on which visitors walk is 313 feet above sea level. Six feet below is the concrete slab that serves as a floor for the memorial trees and a ceiling for the belowground museum spaces.

8

BUILDING BACK

A MONTH BEFORE the fifth anniversary of 9/11, the highly anticipated construction work for the memorial and museum commenced. Heavy machinery descended the ramp into the pit to begin digging the foundations. Amid the protected, shorn-off box column remnants of the original twin towers, workers drilled and blasted into bedrock, already 70 feet below street level, creating holes up to 10 feet deeper. Nearly 150 new footings were created to support the installation of tremendous steel columns from which the memorial would rise. The work marked a true turning point for a project that had faced and surmounted considerable challenges related to budget, design, and competing visions for the site, fiercely held through force of emotion.

I and my sons, Ryan and Dylan Moran, live less than a mile from the nursery . . . where the oak trees for the 9/11 Memorial have been growing for the last four years. We drive past them almost daily. My boys and I feel very blessed to have these beautiful white oak trees growing so close to us. You see, we have always thought of my husband John as a mighty oak tree, just like the trees you are planting at the WTC.

KIMBERLY MORAN-RACKLIN
WHOSE HUSBAND, JOHN MICHAEL MORAN,
AN FDNY BATTALION CHIEF, DIED ON 9/11

Even as construction began, pressures mounted as officials struggled to coordinate the overlapping work on more than a half dozen megaprojects at the World Trade Center site. Within the space of a few city blocks, construction was proceeding on five major skyscrapers housing over ten million square feet of office space, the third largest transportation hub in New York City, preparation for a performing arts center, a new shopping venue, a vehicle screening center, two new city streets, and pedestrian thruways—in addition to the memorial and museum. All of these buildings required that infrastructure such as utilities and communication networks be woven throughout the 16 acres.

Further complicating the construction were two train systems—the Port Authority Trans-Hudson (PATH) from New Jersey and the number 1 New York City Transit subway that cut right through the middle of the site. Continued service was mandated for the 150,000 commuters who relied daily on these train lines. Because a portion of the

memorial's south pool would rest on top of the PATH tracks, tremendous engineering challenges had to be tackled.

Construction scheduling is always a complex challenge among the various trades working on a single project. At the World Trade Center, that complexity multiplied exponentially and required intense daily coordination among the projects. Deliveries of equipment, materials, steel, concrete, the movement of cranes—all needed synchronized management by the Port Authority to keep the multiple projects advancing on schedule. As Lou Mendes, 9/11 memorial vice president of design and construction noted, "To build a job on top of an active railroad is already complicated, then you add all the stakeholders,

the logistics—people have no idea the amount of engineering that needs to be coordinated."

The memorial and museum shared infrastructure with other projects planned for the World Trade Center—including a chiller plant capable of pumping Hudson River water at 30,000 gallons a minute to create cool, dehumidified air for the museum, the transportation hub, pedestrian passageways, and shopping concourses. In some places, the memorial shared structural steel with other projects, and around the site the beams of one building intersected or were layered on top of one another. Christopher O. Ward, who was appointed executive director of the Port Authority in 2008, likened the World Trade Center construction project to a game of pick-up sticks. Construction schedules for one project could not help but have impacts on others going on at the site.

Like many workers on site, the hard hat of construction worker Salvatore Molluzzo (opposite) is decorated with stickers.

Construction workers Randy Rolon, Harry Fiore, and Nelson Martinez (above) pause from the process of waterproofing the plaza in front of 1 World Trade Center, rising in the background.

Every carefully selected memorial tree acclimated in a New Jersey nursery for years before being planted, doted on by arborists who ensured they were meticulously watered, fertilized, and pruned.

Although the final memorial plaza stands at street level, it in fact required the construction of an enormous roof erected 70 feet above an eight-acre underground complex within which workcrews were installing the museum's exhibition spaces, loading bays, passageways, the transportation hub's concourse, train tracks, and cooling equipment. Furthermore, that roof had to carry the weight of hundreds of trees and the two largest man-made waterfalls in North America.

Landscape architect Peter Walker had begun the search for 416 oak trees for the memorial in 2005. Each tree was hand-selected from nurseries within a 500-mile radius of the World Trade Center site, including New York, Pennsylvania, and near Arlington County, Virginia, to honor the three 9/11 attack sites.

The landscape architects and their arborists selected only the sturdiest trees—straight trunks, five-inch diameter, no more than 20 feet tall. These trees had to survive not only the move to the World Trade Center site but also the less-than-ideal conditions during the ongoing construction of the other buildings.

In the spring of 2007, the selected trees were all transported to a nursery in Millstone Township, New Jersey, 40 miles from New York. Individually boxed in large wooden planters, the trees were set in perfectly symmetrical rows in a large open field where they would grow for the next four years.

The nursery's proximity to lower Manhattan allowed the trees to develop in a climate with wind and temperature conditions similar to their future home. Each tree was tagged and numbered so that its growth and care could be tracked. "They each have their own character, their own habits and idiosyncrasies," said Jason Bond, the arborist who tended to the daily, individualized needs of the trees. "We're so much like trees that we don't even know it." As the trees developed, their young branches were carefully pruned so that they would mature to create the effect of a gothic arch when planted in rows on the memorial.

> The trees are really the device that move you from the city into the memorial. These are sacred trees.
>
> **PETER WALKER**
> 9/11 MEMORIAL LANDSCAPE ARCHITECT

CONSTRUCTION PROCEEDED at the site, together with the careful preservation of components of the original World Trade Center buildings. To prevent any damage by heavy machinery, workers covered the box column remnants demarcating the perimeter of the towers' footprints in bedrock. Engineers worked to preserve a section of the original slurry wall in keeping with Daniel Libeskind's master plan. A portion of the wall, measuring 62 feet wide and 64 feet high, was slated for exhibition in an expansive underground hall in the Memorial Museum.

As the site filled with steel beams and columns, it could no longer be called a "pit." By December 2008, the 460-foot ramp that had initially enabled recovery and construction workers to access the base of the site had to be removed. Over the years, that ramp had taken on emotional significance, because it was also the means by which thousands of victims' family members could descend to bedrock on every 9/11 anniversary to lay flowers on the ground where their loved ones were killed. Many dignitaries, including Pope Benedict XVI and 2008 United States presidential candidates Barack Obama and John McCain, had descended the ramp to pay their respects.

Dismantling of the ramp signaled another real milestone. The space it had occupied was soon filled with steel for the memorial's south pool, and now

Portions of the redeveloped World Trade Center are built directly atop active train tracks for the PATH train between New York and New Jersey, just one of the many challenges engineers and construction workers faced as the new site formed.

bedrock at the World Trade Center would not be accessible on the 9/11 anniversaries until the Memorial Museum opened. Architectural plans for the museum included a sloped path for visitors, recalling the processional experience of descending the ramp and entering into a sacred space.

Although the memorial is designed for remembrance and reflection, the museum fulfills the need for historic preservation and education, not only portraying history through its exhibitions but also featuring the remaining archaeological assets of the World Trade Center site—such as the slurry wall and the towers' column remnants—as elements of its architectural design.

Because the memorial sits on top of the primary exhibition galleries, it creates the architectural envelope for the museum, to be filled with artifacts related to the events of 9/11 and exhibits displaying the personal stories behind these events.

A historical exhibition recounts the events of 9/11; covers the antecedents to the attacks, including the 1993 World Trade Center bombing; and explores their ongoing implications. The historical exhibition occupies the footprint of the north tower, while a memorial exhibition to honor the life of every victim is contained within the footprint of the south tower.

Given the memorial's construction schedule, some of the World Trade Center's largest artifacts—including fire trucks and a section of the north tower's antenna—needed to be placed by crane in the exhibition space at bedrock before the memorial plaza covered over the museum as its roof. These key artifacts were so large that construction had to proceed around them.

The concrete remnants known as the "Survivors' Stairs" were built into their final location early on. In July 2008, a crane carefully lowered the 57-ton structure,

Objects take on meaning over time. The ramp has represented not only the physical but the emotional connection between the very bedrock where the events took place and the city—and the world—that surrounds it.

JOE DANIELS

PRESIDENT & CEO, NATIONAL SEPTEMBER 11 MEMORIAL & MUSEUM, THE *NEW YORK TIMES*, DECEMBER 9, 2008

Steel artifacts from the World Trade Center, including the iconic piece known as "the cross," are displayed in the 9/11 Memorial Museum.

It is our hope that the exhibition design in concert with the authentic physicality of the site will speak eloquently to the foundations of resilience, hope, and community on which we, in this post-9/11 world, must build our collective future.

ALICE M. GREENWALD
DIRECTOR, 9/11 MEMORIAL MUSEUM, 2010

21 feet high and 64 feet long, into the site. Work crews later permanently installed it in a location designed so that museum visitors walk alongside it as they descend to the exhibition's lowest levels.

A few weeks before the eighth anniversary of 9/11, the artifact called the "Last Column" returned to the site in a quiet procession flanked by Port Authority Police, NYC Fire Department, and NYC Police Department vehicles. The 58-ton steel column, complete with tribute messages and graffiti still affixed to it from during recovery efforts, had been preserved along with other World Trade Center artifacts in an airplane hangar at John F. Kennedy International

The Survivors' Stairs once connected the elevated Tobin Plaza to Vesey Street. Before plans to include them in the Memorial Museum were finalized, advocacy for their preservation landed the stairs a place on the National Trust for Historic Preservation's list of "America's 11 most endangered historic places."

Airport (JFK). Construction workers spent four hours positioning a crane to lift and transfer the column to bedrock. Wrapped and boxed to protect it from the elements, the Last Column was lowered 70 feet and placed upright on a new footing. Above it, an 88-foot-long, 11.5-foot-deep truss, now carries the load of the Memorial Plaza above, providing headroom, so the Last Column can stand sentry in front of the preserved slurry wall.

Later, other artifacts that had been housed at the JFK hangar were returned for installation in the museum. Two of the steel tridents—forked structural members from the facade of the north tower—returned to the site several days before the ninth anniversary of the attacks. Approximately five stories tall and over 50 tons each, the tridents were too large to travel in one piece; they came

VOICES

JOE DANIELS
President & CEO of the National September 11 Memorial & Museum

"After 9/11, there was such a desire to do something. You could see it on people's faces all over—the impulse to try and make things that little bit better. Donating clothing for recovery workers, cheering on first responders that sped down 'Hero Highway,' sometimes it was just the need to be nicer to folks that somehow, now, weren't total strangers. We were in it, all of us—together.

No doubt that the level of unity wasn't constant over the years, but that was OK, that's expected. The differing opinions and voices and debates, it was passionate because people recognized the importance of 'getting it right' on perhaps the most sacred ground in the United States.

When we started erecting steel on the memorial and work began to accelerate—the commitment I saw on the faces of the construction workers brought me right back to that feeling so widespread after 9/11. Working at ground zero wasn't just an ordinary job, and building this memorial for all of us was a sacred trust we took so seriously.

There were two things that I and the mayor, and everyone on the memorial's board of directors, knew: one, that on the tenth anniversary of the attacks, like it or not, the entire world would be looking to us and that we needed to deliver a memorial that our city and country could be proud of and second, that because of the deep emotional commitment of everyone involved, we would be ready to meet that date. "

AS WORLD TRADE CENTER construction progressed, 7 WTC at the north of the site—the first tower rebuilt after

9/11—became one of the best places from which to see the projects taking shape.

Before its ceremonial removal from ground zero in May 2002, the "Last Column" (above) became an icon of the recovery effort, covered from top to base in photographs, mementos, and remembrances written in spray paint.

On August 24, 2009 (right), first responders watched as ironworkers reinstalled the Last Column in its permanent museum location.

in two pieces and were welded back together on the site. Steel and glass for the museum's pavilion would have to be built around the towering tridents.

■
 ■

BY THE SPRING OF 2010, the memorial pools were fully framed in steel. Concrete pouring had already begun. The 9/11 Memorial staff monitored the progress daily from their offices on the 20th floor of a building across from the site. When complete, the amount of steel for the memorial and museum would equal 8,151 tons, or more than what was used to build the Eiffel Tower in Paris. According to the Port Authority, the amount of concrete would equal 49,900 cubic yards—enough to pave more than 200 miles of New York City sidewalks.

After sections of the concrete-lined plaza were waterproofed, landscaping began. The enormous rooftop garden had to be created in stages to keep the project on schedule for the September 2011 opening of the memorial. Workers built a suspended planting and paving system designed by Peter Walker and Partners that could irrigate and sustain hundreds of trees. A series of precast concrete tables sits on top of soil five feet deep, allowing the tree roots to grow in soil uncompacted by the weight of the plaza. The landscaping design supports the trees throughout the year by recycling rain and snowmelt for its irrigation system.

By the summer of 2010, thousands of pounds of structural soil lay piled in 15-foot mounds at the site in preparation for the arrival of the first trees. In August, 16 trees traveled from the nursery in New Jersey—at night to avoid New York City traffic—resting gently on their sides on flatbed trucks. From midnight through the early morning hours, each tree was installed by crane into its individual trough. By dawn, a swath of greenery dotted a space in between the two memorial pools. New life had returned to the World Trade Center.

Over the years of planning, nearly every aspect of the memorial had been tested, fine-tuned, and perfected. Two full-size sectional mock-ups of the 30-foot waterfalls were created—one in 2005, in the backyard of Toronto-based fountain designer, Dan Euser, and another in 2009, at the Brooklyn Navy Yard, across the East River from ground zero. During these design trials, planners and consultants examined every aspect of the waterfalls. The inside edge of the memorial pools was designed as a comblike weir with grooves

Each memorial swamp white oak tree lived in its own box for four to five years before being installed by crane on the plaza.

The sound of the waterfalls helps create a space separate and apart from the rest of downtown. Finding a peaceful place for reflection is not easy to do in a city as busy as New York. The water helps to define this special space.

CHRISTINE A. FERER

WHOSE HUSBAND, NEIL DAVID LEVIN, EXECUTIVE DIRECTOR OF THE PORT AUTHORITY OF NEW YORK AND NEW JERSEY, DIED ON 9/11

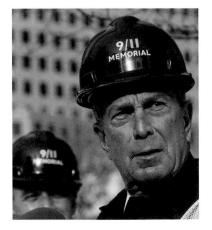

Mayor Michael R. Bloomberg (above) addressed workers on site as construction on the memorial and museum progressed.

A waterfall mock-up built in Brooklyn (opposite) allowed designers to calibrate the appearance of the falling water in the pools.

that shaped the droplets falling into the fountain. Arad envisioned a veil of tears beading the pools' sides rather than clinging walls of water. A second fountain system forms the 20-foot water walls that pour into the inner voids of each pool.

No matter how well designs or models represented the fountains, not until the water was flowing through them at the Memorial Plaza was everyone sure how well they would work. By November 2010, the pumps needed to circulate 26,000 gallons of water through the north pool's waterfalls every minute were installed and ready for testing. It took 12 hours to fill the 18-inch-deep moats around the upper edges of the pool, and then the water was ready to begin falling into the void where the north tower once stood.

As the water flowed over the edges, distinct droplets cascaded down the smooth, dark gray granite panels that lined the interior of the pool. Concerns that wind and pressure from the pumps might create more of a torrent than a gentle fall of water were allayed. The test also confirmed for Michael Arad and memorial planners that the sound of the waterfalls would not be overpowering but would rather provide the tranquillity that Arad had always envisioned and add to the feeling of a contemplative space distinct from the bustle of lower Manhattan. Rainbows created by the sun glistened in the mist of the waterfalls.

Fabrication of the most important feature of the memorial—the bronze panels containing the victims' names—began in mid-2010. Each half-inch-thick panel, weighing approximately 1,000 pounds, was incised by a powerful water-jet cutting machine. After the names were cut and necessary counters applied to fill the voids of letters, bronze workers labored by hand to give the panels their patina. A heating and cooling system was designed to keep the panels warm enough in the winter to melt snow and ice and cool enough in the summer so that people could comfortably run their fingers over the names.

SURVIVOR TREE

THE NYC DEPARTMENT
*of Parks & Recreation
nursed the Survivor Tree
back to health in Van Cort-
landt Park in the Bronx. In
March 2010, a pair of severe
and windy storms uprooted
the tree. Workers initially
worried for the pear tree's
survival, but it ultimately
lived up to its name.*

Weeks after the attacks, amid the wreckage at ground zero, workers discovered a Callery pear tree with charred bark, snapped roots, and branches
reduced to stumps. The tree was originally planted in the 1970s, near the 4 and
5 WTC buildings. When New York City Parks & Recreation Department staff res-
cued the battered tree and brought it to a park in the Bronx, it measured eight feet.
Over the years, the tree began to flourish with careful attention from Parks Department staff, and grew to 30 feet in height, sprouting new branches and flowering in
the springtime. In December 2010, several 9/11 survivors joined Mayor Bloomberg
to mark the tree's return home when it was planted on the plaza of the 9/11 Memorial. Standing tall among the grove of oak trees, the pear tree is a reminder of the
thousands of survivors who persevered after the attacks.

IN 2008 THE PORT AUTHORITY conducted a comprehensive assessment of the construction schedules for every World Trade Center project. Mayor Bloomberg, together with his deputy mayor for economic development, Robert Lieber, the memorial's president Joe Daniels, and many victims' families, stressed the need to open the memorial in time for the tenth anniversary of the attacks. Already, millions of people—victims' family members, survivors, first responders, and visitors from all over the world—were making the pilgrimage to ground zero, gazing through construction fencing at the progress underway and eagerly awaiting the completion of the project. The city, the country, and the world yearned for the hole to be filled.

September 11, 2011, is the only goal that matters, and for the next 306 days we will continue to keep our heads down and locked in on delivering the sacred heart of the site.

CHRISTOPHER O. WARD
EXECUTIVE DIRECTOR, PORT AUTHORITY
OF NEW YORK AND NEW JERSEY,
NEW YORK TIMES, NOVEMBER 10, 2010

Thanks to a combination of public and private funds raised by the memorial board of directors and staff, the project had the necessary financing in place. A grant from the LMDC of U.S. Department of Housing and Urban Development funds allocated in 2005, as well as funds from the State of New York through former Governor Pataki in 2006, made up the public commitment. Additionally, from 2005 to 2008 the 9/11 Memorial raised over $350 million privately, from both large corporations—a number of which had lost employees on 9/11—and from philanthropists, foundations, and hundreds of thousands of people from all 50 states and 38 countries. Fund-raising continues to support the museum's exhibitions and the operations of the memorial and museum, and the LMDC remained a key supporter, with additional funding allocated in 2010 under its chairman, Avi Schick, and president, David Emil, to help build museum exhibitions.

Chairman of the 9/11 Memorial board of directors Mayor Michael R. Bloomberg, center, and President Joe Daniels, left, observed progress on the site, accompanied by news anchor Robin Roberts.

IN JANUARY 2011, on the seven-year anniversary of the day that the memorial jury selected "Reflecting Absence," the jury members visited the World Trade Center to view the project's construction progress and walk its plaza, which was covered in a blanket of snow. Memorial jury member First Deputy Mayor Patricia E. Harris commented that "seeing the design being realized is

A **PORTION** of the slurry wall that kept the Hudson River from flooding lower Manhattan after 9/11 is displayed in

the museum. The wall has been reinforced with a concrete liner wall and new steel tiebacks, anchored into bedrock.

Great memorials cause you to think and to remember, to reflect, and to walk away determined to make sure that some tragedy like this doesn't happen again. And if this memorial can do that, then I think it will have been worth the time and the money and all of the people around the world who contributed to this. Thousands and thousands of people, some gave big donations, some gave small donations, but they all gave their hearts.

MICHAEL R. BLOOMBERG

108TH MAYOR OF THE CITY OF NEW YORK AND
CHAIR OF THE 9/11 MEMORIAL, OCTOBER 26, 2010

breathtaking. You can feel its power even as it is being built."

Construction proceeded six days a week to ensure the plaza could open on the tenth anniversary, with the full support of New York Governor Andrew Cuomo, who took office in January 2011. Because the plaza's northeast corner lies over the transit hub's mezzanine, that portion would wait to be completed later, as work on the hub advanced. Meanwhile, preparation for the museum continued with content and design planning, and new acquisitions to the permanent collection.

In their initial design statement, Michael Arad and Peter Walker envisioned that "the memorial grounds [will] not be isolated from the rest of the city; they will be a living part of it." In keeping, the memorial provides both a place for contemplation and also an up-close encounter with an evolving World Trade Center, including rising towers and a soaring-winged transportation hub. The memorial weaves into the fabric of a living and ever changing city.

In the years since the 9/11 attacks, the World Trade Center has been transformed from a site of an atrocity to a place of recovery, then rebuilding, and finally healing and hope. The memorial overcame years of conflict, differences of opinions, and residual anguish from the tragedy. Some may lament that the rebuilding process was cumbersome and slow, but the difficult steps taken are evidence of democracy at work.

The memorial represents a fulfillment of the collective obligation to remember the victims and to reaffirm a respect for life. At its core, the memorial is a place of remembrance. Because remembering entails looking back, we sometimes mistakenly think of it as belonging in the past. But the National September 11 Memorial is for the here and now—for the grieving to find a path to healing. And it points us toward the future; as a testament to both our loss and our strength, it will stand proud for generations to come.

The rebuilt World Trade Center site (rendering, opposite) is both tribute to the original and a destination of its own. Set within it, the 9/11 Memorial will welcome millions of annual visitors for years to come.

BUILDING THE MEMO

1 **Callery pear tree,** known as the "Survivor Tree," stands on the Memorial Plaza.

2 **Nearly acre-size pools** sit on the footprints of the original towers.

3 **Number of times** the 57-ton Survivors' Staircase needed to be moved so that it could be installed permanently within the museum.

5 **Hours,** approximately, to cut each bronze panel for the memorial.

8 **Hours,** approximately, for two workers to hand-patina each bronze panel to a consistent finish.

8 **Acres of land** occupied by the memorial and museum.

16 **Pumps** power the memorial waterfalls.

30 **Height, in feet,** of the memorial waterfalls.

45 **Seconds, on average,** to water-jet cut each letter on the memorial panels.

60 **Height, in feet,** of the memorial oak trees when they are fully mature.

RIAL BY THE NUMBERS

Height, in feet, of the memorial plaza above foundation level of the World Trade Center site. **70**

Approximate length, in feet, of each side of the memorial pools. **200**

Weight, in pounds, of each 2.5-foot-by-5-foot granite panel that lines the interior of the memorial pools. **420**

Oak trees tagged and selected for the memorial. An overstock was created in case a tree failed to thrive. **437**

Construction workers, approximately, on the memorial and museum project during peak construction. **500**

Names on the memorial. **2,983**

Granite panels lining the interior of each memorial pool. **3,968**

Tons of structural steel used in the memorial and museum. The Eiffel Tower was built with 8,046 tons of structural steel. **8,151**

Cubic yards of concrete used to build the memorial. **50,000**

Gallons of water held in each memorial pool. **485,919**

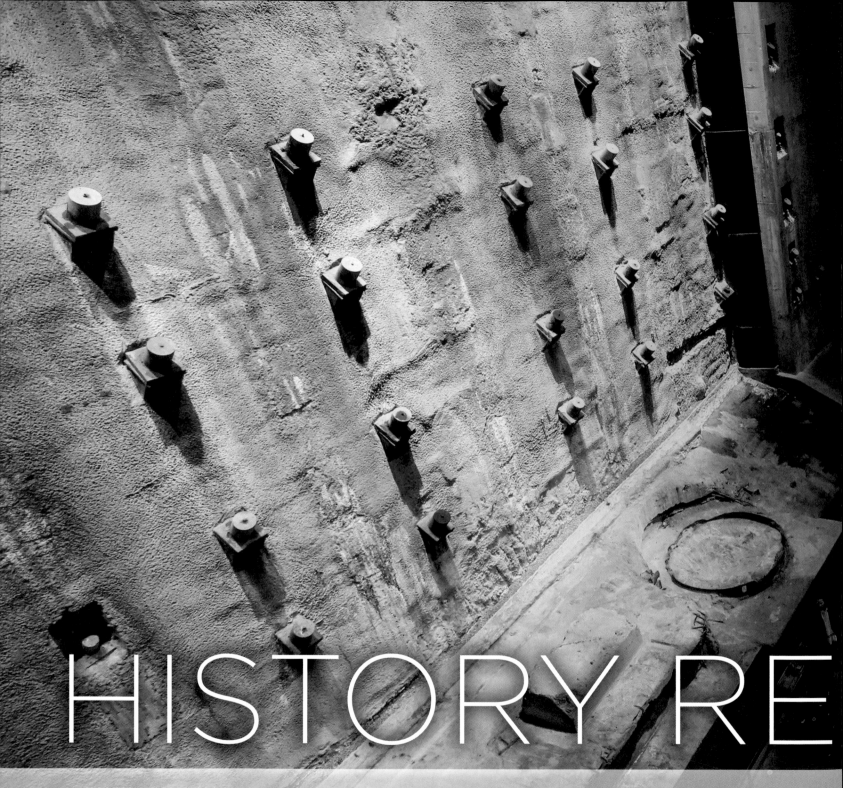

HISTORY RE

MEMBERED

largest space and houses two major artifacts—the World Trade Center slurry wall and the Last Column.

TWO WORLD TRADE CENTER TRIDENTS stand sentry in the museum's atrium, illuminated at night.

9

HOPE REBUILT

THE 9/11 MEMORIAL'S opening on the tenth anniversary of September 11, 2001, fulfilled an essential element of the collective promise to honor and remember those who were killed. The 9/11 Memorial Museum, which was developed simultaneously with the memorial, fulfills the other half of that promise: telling the authoritative history of 9/11, documenting its precursors, and exploring its ongoing implications.

The creation of the 110,000-square-foot museum was led by 9/11 Memorial Chairman Michael R. Bloomberg, President Joe Daniels, Museum Director Alice M. Greenwald, and a team of curators, educators, exhibition developers and designers, architects, and construction professionals. In 2006, the team began to form conceptual plans that would guide the museum's development

Most museums are buildings that house artifacts. Our museum is housed within an artifact.

ALICE GREENWALD
9/11 MEMORIAL MUSEUM DIRECTOR

immediately following key design changes to both the memorial and museum that would define the space and direction of the two components.

The Norwegian architecture firm Snøhetta designed the museum's pavilion, a unique, angular structure that spans a complex network of belowground structures. Nestled between the two memorial pools, the low, horizontally tilting building contrasts with the towering verticality of the skyscrapers surrounding the plaza. Craig Dykers, principal of Snøhetta, described the pavilion's changing reflective, angular surface as creating brightness and a sense of optimism. According to Snøhetta's design intentions, "The building is at once dynamic and tranquil, delicate and rugged, clear and indirect. The architecture is meant to challenge us to accept those often-indefinable dualities and conflicting traits that make all societies human."

The most important elements defining the museum's architectural design were the archaeological remnants of the original World Trade Center, including the box column remnants that outline the two footprints of the twin towers and the slurry wall that holds back the Hudson River. The commitment to preserve these World Trade Center remnants in situ, as required by federal preservation law, resulted in the location of exhibition spaces at bedrock level, 70 feet below the plaza. This design challenge presented an extraordinary opportunity for history to be learned where it happened. The architects of the below-grade portion of the museum, Davis Brody Bond, explained in their design statement: "The nature of the museum is such that the shell of the space, comprising existing foundations, the slurry wall and other in-situ elements of the site is as much an artifact of 9/11 as the contents of the exhibit galleries and casework."

A section of the north tower's steel façade from floor 93 to floor 96 illustrates the force of hijacked Flight 11 when it struck the building, twisting and shredding the steel.

THE ARCHAEOLOGY OF THE SITE was far from the only challenge museum designers confronted. Planners were keenly focused on the world in which the museum was being created: the visitors who would bring their own experiences of 9/11, the technological requirements of exhibitions depicting the most widely documented historical moment of our time, and physical artifacts

RAMON SUAREZ
April 6, 1956–September 11, 2001

VIEW MORE
PLAY PROFILE
CLOSE

RAMON
SUAREZ

SEARCH   ABOUT

ranging in size from a wedding ring to towering scorched steel and fire trucks. The exhibition spaces also needed to be carefully planned in relation to the NYC Office of Chief Medical Examiner's remains repository in a way that would honor that sacred space in perpetuity.

In developing the content of the museum, planners agreed on a four-pronged goal: to create a place for commemoration, preservation, education, and inspiration. Among the earliest tasks in the planning process was identifying the museum's audience. Museum planners had to consider local, national, and international visitors, as well as those with no firsthand knowledge of 9/11, including future generations. In a 2010 essay for *Curator: The Museum Journal,* Greenwald explained that "at its core, the memorial museum must carefully balance the act of commemoration—which has its own requirements of

Touch tables enable visitors to discover additional information about the individuals commemorated in the memorial exhibition, including photographs, images of objects, and oral remembrances by loved ones.

The Ladder Company 3 truck, located outside the historical exhibition in Center Passage, was led by highly decorated Captain Patrick "Paddy" John Brown. Eleven of the company's members responded to the World Trade Center on September 11, 2001, and perished that day.

sensibility and reverence—with the imperatives of education, historical documentation, and fidelity to the emotionally resonant artifacts on display." The delicate balance between commemoration and education was further shaped by the museum's location at the very site where the attacks occurred.

To help navigate these challenges and inform the exhibition planning, Greenwald convened a Museum Planning Conversation Series. Over the course of eight years (2006–2013), the series brought together representatives of key stakeholder groups including victims' family members, survivors, first responders, the lower Manhattan community, and government officials, as well as leading experts on museums, memorialization, and collective trauma. During the sessions, stakeholders grappled with difficult issues and shared opinions and concerns regarding a wide variety of topics, including decisions surrounding the use of explicit imagery and artifacts within the exhibitions.

In an early session, historian Edward T. Linenthal spoke to the group about the inevitable debates and controversies that would ensue as the museum plans formed. He assured the group that "controversy doesn't mean that something's wrong; it means that people are passionately engaged."

Museum staff also consulted with a diverse group of museum professionals, historians, academics, interfaith leaders, historic preservationists, and focus groups with victims' families, survivors, and rescue and recovery workers. Given the nature of the history, challenging decisions had to be made regarding how to convey what happened through objective, engaging, and comprehensive exhibitions. The most sensitive and charged design and content proposals were brought to the 9/11 Memorial board's program committee, a group of 9/11 family members and cultural leaders.

Although planners were committed to ensuring the museum would present an objective and comprehensive historical account of the events, they knew that certain material was particularly intense and needed to be handled with added sensitivity. Understanding some visitors might not be willing or emotionally able to encounter excruciating parts of this story, planners decided to create alcoves to sequester sensitive content, allowing visitors to make a choice whether to view a specific exhibition section or bypass it. Among such heartrending parts of the museum's historical exhibition is the unimaginable situation faced by so many individuals who jumped or fell to their death from the towers. This emotional piece of the history of 9/11 is both crucial and sensitive, and as such is presented in an alcove that gives visitors the choice of whether to view the content.

Some decisions about content caused public controversy and elicited debate. When the museum design team included in a presentation the plan for images of the 9/11 hijackers to be part of the exhibition, some 9/11 families strongly argued that their inclusion would be disrespectful to the memory of their loved ones. Many others, however, were staunchly committed to providing a comprehensive account of the attacks, which meant presenting an accurate record of the 9/11 plot—including the identities of the 19 hijackers and Osama bin Laden. Planners decided to address the rise of al Qaeda and the hijackers in

Responding to terrorism is both a challenge to our core values and an opportunity to act on them.

MUSEUM PROGRAM COMMITTEE

GUIDING PRINCIPLES DOCUMENT, APRIL 2008

The third part of the historical exhibition tells the story of the aftermath of 9/11—including the recovery efforts at the attack sites. Among the artifacts on display is a Department of Sanitation hard hat worn by Salvatore Annerino, who led an emergency response division at ground zero.

Now there will be children born after 9/11, who only read about that day in books. Some of them might even think the people it happened to weren't real. But we are here to help them know that they were.

JAMES LAYCHAK

PENTAGON MEMORIAL FUND PRESIDENT,
WHOSE BROTHER DAVID W. LAYCHAK
WAS KILLED ON 9/11

the exhibitions, citing the importance of making a clear statement about who was responsible for the horrific crimes and reinforcing that these were indefensible acts of human agency. As 9/11 Memorial President Joe Daniels explained, "There can be no mistake that the 9/11 attacks were neither plane accidents nor natural disasters—they were caused by heartless murderers who sought to terrorize our country."

WHILE THE CREATION of the museum's exhibitions advanced offsite in conference rooms, designer studios, and fabricator workshops, other challenges complicated the construction effort—including engineering puzzles, funding disputes with surrounding World Trade Center projects, and damage resulting from Superstorm Sandy. On the eve of the 9/11 anniversary in 2012, the 9/11 Memorial and the Port Authority of New York and New Jersey made an agreement to move toward the museum's completion. Under the leadership of Mayor Bloomberg, New York Governor Andrew Cuomo, and New Jersey Governor Chris Christie, a disagreement over the project's funding structure was resolved, enabling the building to proceed to an opening in the spring of 2014.

By 2011, the exterior of the museum's entry pavilion, the aboveground structure, had been substantially completed and clad in shining metal and reflective glass surfaces. Two World Trade Center tridents stood sentry in its glass atrium, illuminated at night and visible to memorial visitors. Recovered from the north tower, the tridents recalled the distinctive Gothic arch motif of the twin towers, and as markers of the gateway to the museum they conveyed central themes of the 9/11 story—survival, resilience, strength, and hope.

In addition to serving as the entry point to the largely belowground museum, the pavilion was designed to include an auditorium, a café, and a private room for victims' families. For more than 12 years a temporary family room was

The pavilion's exterior is composed of glass and metal cladding, creating varying reflective surfaces. The striated-metal design is reminiscent of the facade of the twin towers.

IN 2002, Brookfield Properties donated a private space overlooking the World Trade Center site for victims' families.

Over the years, families left thousands of items of remembrance, filling the room from floor to ceiling with tributes.

ABOUT **8:30**AM
SEPTEMBER 11, 2001

LOWER MANHATTAN,
VIEW FROM BROOKLYN

*Photographer David Monderer captured
a view of lower Manhattan (above) from
Brooklyn at about 8:30 a.m. on September
11, 2001. The image is seen at the start of
the introductory exhibition.*

*The historical exhibition tells the story of the
Flight 93 passengers and crew who tried
to overtake the aircraft from the hijackers.
Among the objects recovered at the crash
site were a wristwatch (opposite) and a
business card belonging to passenger Todd
Beamer. The date on the watch still reads 11.*

located on the 20th floor of One Liberty Plaza overlooking the World Trade Center site. Over time, the walls and even the windows of the room had become papered with photographs, cards, and letters filled with heartbreaking and loving expressions of grief. One woman who lost her son tacked his picture to the wall with a note reading, "To the world he may have been just one person, but to me, he was the world."

Recognizing the sanctity and historical legacy of the One Liberty Plaza Family Room, a committee of family members worked with the 9/11 Memorial and the New York State Museum to plan and design a new room and ensure that the items in the original one would be carefully and respectfully preserved.

Planners sought to develop an experience that transitions visitors from the bright, airy pavilion space into the archaeological heart of the World Trade Center, exploring the events of 9/11 and facilitating an encounter with history that is about tragic loss but also about the triumph of the human spirit.

Descending from the pavilion alongside the tridents, the design takes visitors into a quieter and more contemplative space. Arriving at the concourse lobby level, three stories below the memorial plaza, visitors find themselves between the structures housing the two memorial pools, which are sheathed in an ethereal aluminum material in a soft gesture to the silvery cladding of the twin towers.

From there, Davis Brody Bond designed one of the museum's signature architectural elements—a ramp recalling the one that had served the site during the ground zero recovery. At key points along this new, gently sloping transition, visitors encounter views of the vast spaces below, revealing in situ remnants of the World Trade Center site and historic artifacts. Along the ramped descent to bedrock, Thinc Design, the museum's lead exhibition designer, envisioned an experience that would draw upon "processional aspects of public memorialization: encountering the site, remembering the loss, bearing witness, reconstructing and reflecting." This shared entry experience gives visitors a unified starting point on their journey and then allows them to create their own encounters with history. Thinc Design principal Tom Hennes explained that this technique was meant "to open ourselves empathically to others' experience of 9/11 and to gain new perspectives on our own experience—both through the re-encounter with our memories and through the wider range of experiences represented."

In the final descent to bedrock, visitors pass alongside the Survivors' Stairs and find themselves in Memorial Hall, between the two towers' footprints. The wall connecting those footprints also divides the museum from the private space reserved for the medical examiner's repository of remains. Planners decided to approach several artists and ask them to imagine how this wall could be treated distinctly from the rest of the museum, with appropriate reverence for this deeply important and sacred space. Artist Spencer Finch developed a piece

We often define our history now as the time pre-9/11 and post-9/11. The function of Todd's watch was to tell what time it is. It doesn't do that anymore. What it does tell is what time it was. It says it's the 11th and marks the time that the successful counterattack on Flight 93 ended.

DAVID BEAMER

FATHER OF TODD M. BEAMER, PASSENGER ON FLIGHT 93, SPEAKING ABOUT HIS SON'S WATCH ON DISPLAY IN THE MUSEUM

While searching for survivors on 9/11, NYPD detective Peter Boylan discovered a torn and burned American flag (above) in the rubble. Several other American flags and remnants of tattered flags were recovered from the World Trade Center site.

The Vesey Street stair remnant (right) also known as the historic Survivors' Stairs was the first artifact to be installed in the museum.

entitled "Trying to Remember the Color of the Sky on That September Morning," honoring each of the victims of the attacks through 2,983 individual watercolor squares, each hand-painted a different shade of blue and affixed to an enormous, 40-foot-high grid. The artwork surrounds the Virgil quote forged from World Trade Center steel: "No day shall erase you from the memory of time."

From Memorial Hall, visitors can choose to visit either of the museum's core exhibitions—a historical exhibition entitled "September 11, 2001" and a memorial exhibition called "In Memoriam"—which reside within the north and south tower footprints, respectively. "In Memoriam" aims to honor each victim of the 1993 and 2001 attacks. The exhibit emphasizes the magnitude of loss through a vast corridor of floor-to-ceiling portraits of those killed—but it also focuses on the individuality of each of those victims, presenting cherished memories through a rotating sequence of individual profiles and interactive tables containing photos and remembrances recorded by their loved ones

"September 11, 2001" provides an unfolding historical account of what happened on 9/11, the precursors that led up to that day, and the aftermath, recovery, and ongoing questions and implications that still exist in our world today. Designers developed three primary ways to tell the complex story of the day of the attacks: a time line wrapping the entire exhibit, detailing what

The first part of the historical exhibition recounts the unfolding events on September 11, 2001, through multimedia displays including artifacts such a piece of Flight 11's fuselage.

was happening in the air and on the ground; exhibits presenting digital material and physical artifacts; and alcoves focusing on first-person audio accounts of the history and other sensitive content. David Layman, principal of Layman Design, the historical exhibition designer, noted that "both exhibit and visitor are witnesses to that day, sharing memories each step of the way."

Consideration of the visitor experience was a key driver of design decisions. A number of large artifacts, including the Last Column, were placed in spaces outside the main exhibitions. These locations strengthened the visitor's journey by allowing the objects to be seen from different perspectives at multiple points in the telling of the history. The artifacts' placement also created visual clues allowing for the visitor experience to unfold in an intuitive way.

As a major global event at the start of the 21st century, 9/11 generated an unprecedented amount of media documentation. Local Projects, the museum's media designer, recognized early in the design process that integrating media in all its forms would be essential to successful exhibitions. According to Jake Barton, principal of Local Projects, first-person accounts "lend authenticity to the exhibits, matching the powerful and raw archaeology of the greater museum space." Incorporating audiovisual materials of this nature and scale was groundbreaking. Throughout the museum, voice recordings create

Before the May 15, 2014, Dedication Ceremony, Chairman Michael Bloomberg toured President Barack Obama, First Lady Michelle Obama, former President Bill Clinton, and Hillary Rodham Clinton through the museum. President Obama called the museum a "sacred place of hope and healing" that will ensure that "generations yet unborn will never forget."

Aluminum surfaces on the understructures of the memorial pools (opposite) create an ethereal quality, as if the massive volumes float over the earlier buildings' footprints. The architects intended to create "an abstracted physical reminder of the original tower locations [that] reinforce the visitor's sense of place on the site."

VOICES

CHAIRMAN MICHAEL R. BLOOMBERG

Museum Dedication Ceremony, May 15, 2014

"This museum, built on the site of rubble and ruins, is now filled with the faces, the stories, and the memories of our common grief and our common hope. It is a witness to tragedy. It is an affirmation of human life. It is a reminder to us—and to all future generations—that freedom carries heavy responsibilities. And it is a reflection of our belief that the true hope of humanity resides in our compassion and kindness for one another.

Walking through this museum can be difficult at times. But it is impossible to leave without feeling inspired. Each story here beats with a human heart, which, if we allow it, touches our own. The stories are the proof that what we do, and the choices we make, affect each other's lives and the course of human history."

SPENCER FINCH'S ART INSTALLATION "Trying to Remember the Color of the Sky on That September Morning"

surrounds a quote by Virgil. In December 2014, the Duke and Duchess of Cambridge viewed the expansive work.

SYMBOL OF STRENGTH

Standing tall at the center of the museum's largest open space—the cathedral-like Foundation Hall—is the "Last Column," a 36-foot-tall, 58-ton core column from the south tower that was the last steel remnant from the twin towers to be removed from the site at the end of the nine-month recovery.

In March 2002, remains of six missing members of FDNY Squad 41 were found in the area near the column. To mark the recovery, a squad member spray-painted "SQ 41" on the column. And before long, it became a place for those toiling at ground zero to memorialize their losses and affirm their solidarity through spray-painted graffiti, notes, and prayer cards.

Museum visitors first encounter the Last Column, now re-anchored into bed-rock, near the start of their experience, looking down into Foundation Hall from a ramp that slowly guides them to bedrock, recalling the ramp used in the recovery. They next see it at the end of their museum experience, now from a new perspective: looking up at its majesty from bedrock level, having gained a new understanding of what happened on 9/11 and how the best of humanity shone in response.

THE LAST COLUMN *is complemented by oral histories of those who were involved in the recovery effort.*

visceral connections with visitors, both emotionally and cognitively. The recordings include those of a widow remembering how her husband used to act like a "big kid," a survivor recalling his harrowing escape from the north tower, and a Flight 93 passenger leaving a voice mail telling her family she loved them—and each offers historical documentation that is intimate, compelling, and personal, thereby emphasizing the universality of the human experience. By 2015, the museum had collected well over 2,000 oral recordings, including interviews gathered through the national oral history project StoryCorps.

Staff also made concerted efforts to collect as much physical material as possible to complete the exhibitions and grow the permanent collection. Groups including Voices of September 11th, StoryCorps, and the 9/11 Tribute Center partnered with the museum to provide photographs, mementos, oral recordings, and other material. Museum staff reached out to victims' families, recovery workers, labor unions, private companies, first responder agencies, and cultural institutions to secure critical artifacts and personal effects that could best tell the story in the historical exhibition and other areas of the museum.

Recognizing the importance of capturing firsthand accounts of 9/11 history, museum staff devised multiple strategies to continue to collect messages, stories, and remembrances. Recording booths installed toward the end of the museum visit enable visitors to share their own 9/11 stories, preserve memories of loved ones, or express opinions about issues arising in the wake of the attacks. All of these recordings are added to the museum's archive, and exhibitions are continually updated to include new voices. In Foundation Hall, surrounding the Last Column, visitors can explore and add to registries for 9/11 rescue and recovery workers, survivors and witnesses, and 9/11 memorials around the world. Before leaving the museum, visitors are invited to sign a digital guestbook that projects messages onto a map of the world.

> When I heard that the museum was looking for artifacts, I thought about my shoes . . . I wanted my nieces and my nephew and every person who asks what happened to see them and maybe understand a little better what it felt like to have been us on that day.

FLORENCE JONES
9/11 SURVIVOR WHO ESCAPED FROM
THE 77TH FLOOR OF THE SOUTH TOWER

On 9/11, Florence Jones evacuated the south tower after hijacked Flight 175 struck one floor above her. In the stairwell, the heels became an impediment to a fast exit, so her boss, Carl Boudakian, carried her shoes. She continued downstairs and all the way home in her stocking feet.

TO UNVEIL THE MUSEUM to the world, a televised dedication ceremony highlighted compelling museum stories. 9/11 Memorial chairman and former Mayor Michael R. Bloomberg hosted the ceremony, and present and former elected officials who served at the time of the 9/11 attacks participated in the program. President Barack Obama, New York and New Jersey Governors Andrew Cuomo and Chris Christie, New York City Mayor Bill de Blasio, former Governors George Pataki and Donald DiFrancesco, and former Mayor Rudolph Giuliani spoke alongside family members, survivors, and 9/11 rescue and recovery workers, who shared their 9/11 stories and their hopes for what the museum would mean to future generations. Former President Bill Clinton was among the guests in attendance, along with hundreds of those personally affected by the attacks. The ceremony program showcased the stories behind both monumental and more intimate artifacts presented in the museum, including the Last Column, the Survivors' Stairs, a watch belonging to Flight 93 passenger Todd Beamer, a pair of shoes worn by survivor Florence Jones, and a red bandanna that belonged to 24-year-old Welles Crowther, who died helping others to safety on September 11.

Following the ceremony, the museum stayed open continuously for a 24-hours-a-day stretch, to provide a special opportunity for 9/11 stakeholders to preview the exhibitions during a week-long dedication period. More than 40,000 9/11

VOICES

ALISON CROWTHER

whose son Welles Remy Crowther was killed on 9/11 in the south tower, spoke at the museum dedication ceremony, May 15, 2014

" I am Welles Crowther's mother, Alison Crowther. My husband, Jefferson, and I could not be more proud of our son. For us, he lives on, in the people he helped and in the memory of what he chose to do that Tuesday in September.

Welles believed that we are all connected, as one human family that we are here to look out for, and to care for one another. This is life's most precious meaning.

It is our greatest hope that when people come here and see Welles's red bandanna, they will remember how people helped each other that day. And we hope that they will be inspired to do the same, in ways both big and small.

This is the true legacy of 9/11. "

family members, rescue and recovery workers, first responders, survivors, and lower Manhattan residents and business owners attended the previews.

By the time the museum opened, nearby construction had also reached a critical point. Fences that had separated the site from the public for nearly 13 years could come down. The memorial became an integrated part of lower Manhattan, just as planners had envisioned. On September 11, 2014, thousands of visitors gathered to view the "Tribute in Light" shining into the night sky just south of the memorial.

Together, the 9/11 Memorial and Museum uphold the collective promise to never forget. They provide a place for remembrance, reflection, learning, and inspiration. Millions of people, from all 50 states and countries around the world, have visited the memorial and museum, quickly solidifying this site as an important national tribute and steward of our shared history. And every day, there are moments at this site that recall the way people came together in the aftermath of the attacks—whether families reuniting to place flowers on a loved one's name or strangers gathering in Foundation Hall to recall the heroic recovery effort. All who visit take the time to remember, to learn, and to be inspired to care for one another—and in so doing, they leave with a piece of the mission of the 9/11 Memorial and Museum to carry with them wherever they go.

Welles Remy Crowther, a young trader whose office was located on the South Tower's 104th Floor, helped guide a number of survivors to a stairwell. Some remember him wearing a red bandanna—similar to one of his spares now displayed at the museum (opposite)—over his mouth to protect against smoke. Welles did not survive.

On the 13th anniversary of 9/11, the plaza opened to the general public, allowing a view of "Tribute in Light" from the memorial.

At the start of kindergarten I
witnessed & remember every

This is a
story of slrng

We
wi

The Day

Kindergarden in a NYC public school.
3 of us were left at the end of
the day and playe

SAN FRANCISCO
P.D.

Co. G - NEVER FORGET

GOD BLES

AND HE WILL WIPE OUT EVERY
TEAR FROM THEIR EYES AND
DEATH WILL BE NO MORE.
REVELATIONS 21:4

CLECKLEY

We were mere kids when this
happened. Now as adults we
understand the impact of this
tragic event and respect all
who lost their lives & those who
risked th

T

PROUD TO BE AN
AML

Foreve

Ruth + ?
We Wil
M

8th Grade Scienc
is when I got the ne
standing outside f

Visitors are invited to sign a digital guest book located in Foundation Hall next to a multi-ton World Trade Center steel column. Projected messages overlaid on the signer's country of origin form a world map, demonstrating the shared experience felt by visitors from across the globe and the worldwide impact of 9/11. Left in numerous languages and by people of all ages, the messages are recorded in the museum's digital archives.

SAGES FROM THE WORLD

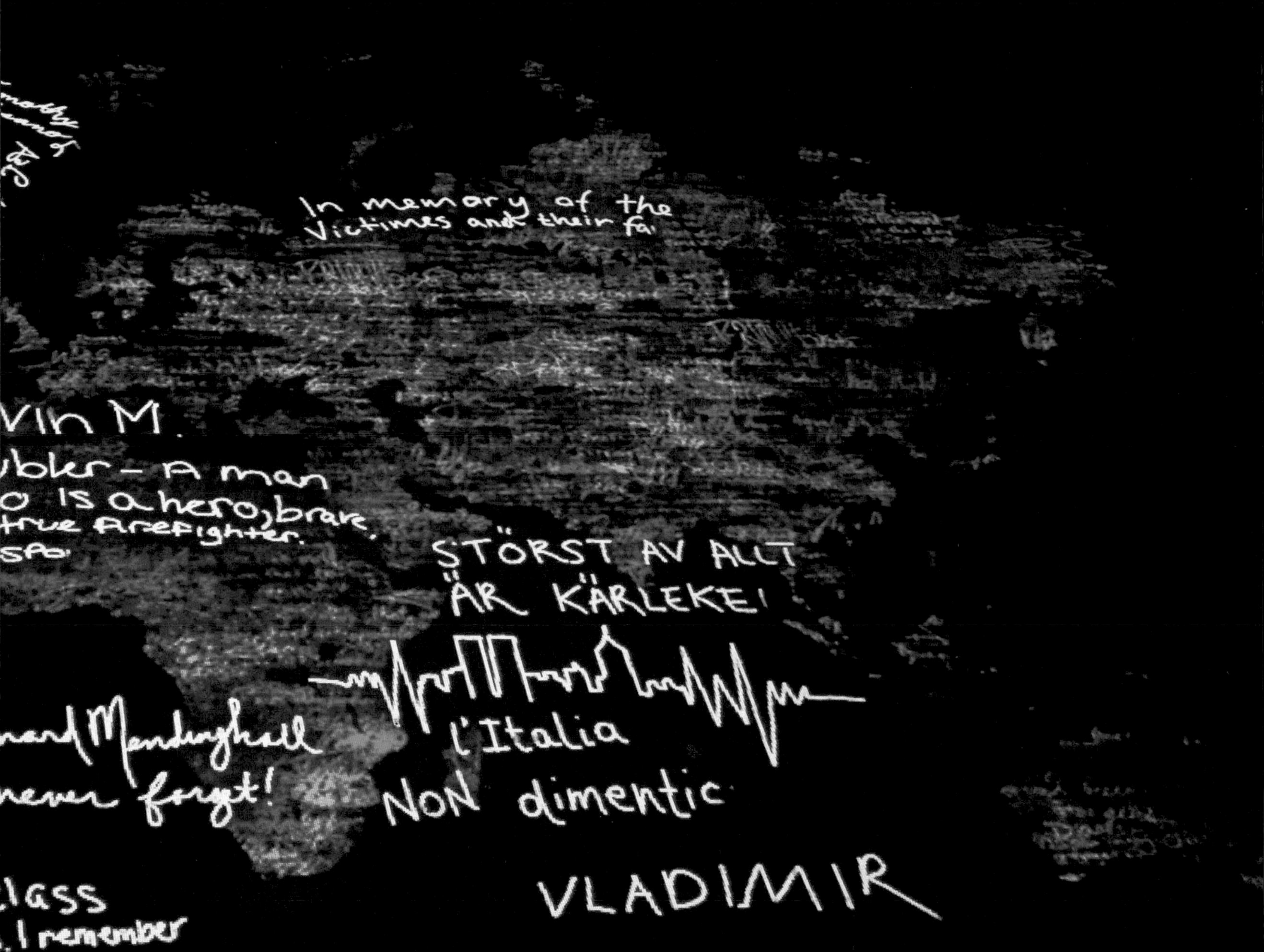

THE FULLY REBUILT World Trade Center site will include many elements of the original complex: commercial, retail,

and public transportation spaces. The National September 11 Memorial is located at its heart, nestled among the new towers.

AFTERWORD

Undertaking the work of building the National September 11 Memorial & Museum has been a privilege of a lifetime. The day-to-day work ranges from the enormous and evolving societal meaning of the attacks to the very emotional and specific efforts that are so personal to individual 9/11 family members. It has allowed me to come to know hundreds of people who care so deeply about building this memorial to the innocent who were so violently taken—a memorial in what forever will be one of the most sacred places in the United States that will show our fellow countrymen and the world that we will not forget what happened here, at the Pentagon, and on that field in Somerset County, Pennsylvania. There are so many reasons people have chosen to contribute to this project: to remember friends lost, to express that this country, "the land of the free and home of the brave," is worth fighting to protect, to preserve a history that simply must be passed down to future generations.

The responsibility to sustain this memorial is one that is shared by all of us. In the same way that the fields of Gettysburg, the beaches of Normandy, and the waters of Pearl Harbor are places that teach each successive generation of Americans about who we are as a nation, the 9/11 Memorial and Museum, built at ground zero itself, will forever be a part of our collective fabric. Every dollar that is donated to us will help ensure that this memorial and museum is cared for with the love, respect, and commitment that befits it.

In 2007, we had the privilege of traveling to cities across the country with steel beams being used in the construction of the 9/11 Memorial. Tens of thousands of people signed the beams with messages of hope and remembrance and resilience. Many of them had their own personal stories about what they experienced on 9/11 or inspiring recollections about what their communities did to help in the aftermath. Equally as powerful was seeing the children, many who were too young to have a specific memory of the attacks, look up into their parents' eyes and simply ask the questions we were all asking: "Why did this happen?" "Who did this to us?" "Who were those people that died?" Seeing those parents, many with tears in their eyes, grapple to answer those questions is an unforgettable reminder about our responsibility to the future.

For me, it comes down in large part to what I saw in the weeks that followed 9/11: the love, compassion, and patriotism that I felt when we came together as a city and a country. I will never forget stepping off the E train's World Trade Center stop at 8:50 a.m. on the morning of 9/11; those images are seared in my mind forever. But I also, thank God, will never forget what I saw standing along the West Side Highway with my wife and total strangers, tears in our eyes, yelling words of encouragement to the first responders and recovery workers on their way to give everything of themselves at ground zero. And I will always remember feeling an almost spiritual connection to my neighbors, to my city, and to those around the world who poured their hearts out in grief and compassion—a connection now forged in the names of the 2,983 people, whom we will never forget.

—JOE DANIELS
President & CEO,
National September 11 Memorial & Museum

ACKNOWLEDGMENTS

There are many staff members from the 9/11 Memorial who contributed to the content of this book, chiefly Joe Daniels, whose leadership on the book and in the larger project has been motivating and inspiring. Alice Greenwald and Jan Ramirez provided guidance and thoughtful reviews. So many others were invaluable in reviewing and advising the work in progress, especially memorial architect Michael Arad. We also thank our partners at StoryCorps and Voices of September 11th, both of which provide crucial content for the museum.

From National Geographic, we want to thank our editor, Susan Tyler Hitchcock, for her wisdom and support throughout this project, as well Melissa Farris for her beautiful design work and Kat Irannejad for her photo editing.

We are indebted to the partners who work with us every day at the Port Authority of New York and New Jersey. We express our extraordinary gratitude and appreciation for our chairman, Michael R. Bloomberg, and the members of his administration as Mayor of the City of New York, including Patricia E. Harris, Robert Steel, Dan Doctoroff, Robert Lieber, Andrew Winters, and Kate D. Levin; New York Governor Andrew M. Cuomo and his staff; former New York Governors George E. Pataki, David A. Paterson, and Eliot Spitzer and their staff; New Jersey Governor Chris Christie; former New Jersey Governors James McGreevey and Jon S. Corzine; the Port Authority and its executive directors during the rebuilding: Joe Seymour, Kenneth J. Ringler, Jr., Anthony Shorris, Christopher O. Ward, and Patrick Foye; the Lower Manhattan Development Corporation; Silverstein Properties; the Empire State Development Corporation and its former chairman, Charles Gargano; and so many others whose hearts are in the rebuilding of lower Manhattan.

We want to thank from the bottom of our hearts all of the family members of victims who, through strength and fortitude, have shared their time, voices, and talents to supporting the causes important to them, each of whom has contributed to the realization of the memorial and museum. Some of these include 9/11 Families for a Safe and Strong America; 9/11 Parents and Families of Firefighters and World Trade Center Victims; the 9/11 Widows' and Victims' Families Association; Advocates for a 9/11 Fallen Heroes Memorial; the Cantor Fitzgerald Relief Fund; the Coalition of 9/11 Families; Families of September 11th; the FDNY Families Advisory Council; Fix the Fund; Give Your Voice; the LMDC Families Advisory Council; MyGoodDeed; Peaceful Tomorrows; September 11th Education Trust; September's Mission; the Skyscraper Safety Campaign; Take Back the Memorial; Tuesday's Children; Voices of September 11th; Windows of Hope; WTC Families for Proper Burial; WTC United Family Group; and the relief organizations started by the corporations that suffered the loss of employees on 9/11.

Throughout the past ten years, so many have played vital roles in the creation of the memorial who could not be mentioned in the space of this book. Some confronted the earliest challenges of choosing a master plan for the site amid a downtown community struggling to recover. Others worked at the drafting tables on the technical creation of every millimeter of the design. Thousands worked on the construction site, many of them having also been part of building the twin towers and helping in the post-9/11 recovery. Though their names are not present in this book, we hope their actions and spirit are fully represented.

Finally, we are grateful to our colleagues at the 9/11 Memorial—each of whom knows this is not "just a job" and has such a deep sense of commitment to those who lost loved ones on 9/11, of patriotism and strength, and hope for the future.

ABOUT THE MEMORIAL

The National September 11 Memorial & Museum is the private not-for-profit organization charged with overseeing the design and construction, raising the necessary funds, and programming and operating the memorial and museum at the World Trade Center site.

Educational programming, exhibitions in the museum, and the ongoing maintenance of the memorial are possible only through donations from generous people around the world. If you are interested in donating to help sustain the mission of the National September 11 Memorial & Museum into the future, please visit the website at *911memorial.org*.

Chairman of the Board
Michael R. Bloomberg, *108th Mayor, City of New York*

Honorary Chairman
George E. Pataki, *53rd Governor, State of New York*

Honorary Board Members

President George H. W. Bush
41st President of the United States

President George W. Bush
43rd President of the United States

President Jimmy Carter
39th President of the United States

President William J. Clinton
42nd President of the United States

CONTRIBUTORS

MICHAEL R. BLOOMBERG *(foreword)* was elected the 108th mayor of the City of New York in 2001. He is the founder of Bloomberg L.P., a financial news and media company with offices in more than 160 countries. He attended Johns Hopkins University and Harvard Business School.

JOE DANIELS *(afterword)* is president of the National September 11 Memorial & Museum. Previously he worked at the Robin Hood Foundation; McKinsey & Company; and Cravath, Swaine & Moore. Daniels studied at the University of Pennsylvania Law School and Washington University.

ALLISON BAILEY BLAIS *(author)* is the chief of staff at the National September 11 Memorial & Museum. She previously worked at the Lower Manhattan Development Corporation. She graduated from Cornell University and earned a master's degree from Columbia University.

LYNN RASIC *(author)* is the executive vice president for external affairs at the National September 11 Memorial & Museum and previously was press secretary to New York governor George Pataki. On 9/11, she was deputy press secretary to New York City mayor Rudolph Giuliani. She graduated from Brown University.

ILLUSTRATIONS CREDITS

Cover, Jin S. Lee; 1, Louis Jawitz/Workbook Stock/Getty Images; 2-3, Jason Edwards; 4, Amy Dreher; 6, Peter Walker Partners; 8-9, Joe Woolhead; 10-11, Joe Woolhead; 12-13, Joe Woolhead; 18-19, Rex A. Stucky; 20, Angelo Horna/Corbis; 22, Stan Wayman/Time Life Pictures/Getty Images; 23, Ed Clarity/NY Daily News Archive/Getty Images; 24-25, Tony Linck/Time Life Pictures/Getty Images; 26 (LE), AP Images/G. Paul Burnett; 26 (RT), Stan Reis; 27, Bettmann/Corbis; 28, Kelly-Mooney Photography/Corbis; 29, AP Images/Alan Welne; 30-31, Frank Hurley/NY Daily News Archive/Getty Images; 32, AP Images/Joe Tabacca; 33, Joseph Martella; 34, Harry Hamburg/NY Daily News Archive/Getty Images; 35, Gift of Jon Weston in memory of my parents; 36 (UP), Gift of Evan Kuz; 36 (LO), James Leynse/Corbis; 37, Kevin Daley; 38-39, Stacy Gold/National Geographic Collection/Getty Images; 40-41, Masatomo Kuriya/Corbis; 42, Spencer Platt/Getty Images; 44, Seth Cohen; 47, Stephen Jaffe/AFP/Getty Images; 48-49, Mark M. Lawrence/Corbis; 50, Steve Mellon/Pittsburgh Post-Gazette/Corbis; 51, Mai/Time Life Pictures/Getty Images; 52, Lyle Owerko/Getty Images; 54 (LE), Mario Tama/Getty Images; 54 (RT), Mario Tama/Getty Images; 55, Neville Elder/Corbis Sygma; 56, Shannon Stapleton/Reuters/Corbis; 57, Ray Stubblebine/Reuters/Corbis; 58-59, Rob Howard/Corbis; 60, Shannon Stapleton/Reuters/Corbis; 61, Neville Elder/Corbis Sygma; 62, Larry Downing/Reuters/Corbis; 63, Yoni Brook/Corbis; 64-65, Hubert Boesl/dpa/Corbis; 66-67, Michael Rieger/Mai/Mai/Time Life Pictures/Getty Images; 68, Preston Keres/US Navy/Getty Images; 70, Michael Rieger/FEMA; 71 (LE), Steve McCurry/Magnum Photos; 71 (RT), Mai/Mai/Time Life Pictures/Getty Images; 72, Gift of Jon Weston in memory of my parents; 73, "The Fathers Eight" photograph by Curtis Quinn; 74-75, Mario Tama/Getty Images; 76, Joe Raedle/Getty Images; 77, Gschaar ID, Two Dollar Bill, Ring and Photo, Gift of Myrta Gschaar in honor of my beloved husband Robert J. Gschaar; 77, Williams ID, Gift of Sherri and Corey Williams, mother and brother of Candace Lee Williams; 77, Photo, Gift of Ester DiNardo; 77, St. Anthony Beads, Cash, Lipstick and Glasses, Gift of Eileen A. Fagan, sister of Patricia Mary Fagan; 77, Note, Gift of Barbara Spence, Kristina Spence, Shannon Spence; 77, Keyboard, Deposited by the Office of Chief Medical Examiner; 77, Scissors, Keys, Knife and Medal, In loving memory from Nina Barnes, sole surviving paternal first cousin; 78, Stan Honda/AFP/Getty Images; 79, Peter Ginter/Science Faction/Corbis; 80, Peter Ginter/Getty Images; 81, Christopher Morris/VII/Corbis; 82, Lynn Johnson/National Geographic/Getty Images; 83, Gift of Jon Weston in memory of my parents; 84-85, Lynn Johnson/National Geographic/Getty Images; 86, Ira Block; 87, Spencer Platt/Getty Images; 88-89, Michael Rieger/FEMA; 90-91, Mural created by the Lower School Art Students of Porter-Gaud School in Charleston, South Carolina, in Mrs. Laura Orvin's Art Class for the people of New York. Gift of Lawrence Knafo; 92, Donald Lokuta; 94, Len Jacobs; 95, Mario Tama/Getty Images; 96, Gift of Dennis and Betty Nielsen and Freedom Quilters for all the 9/11 families; 97 (LE), Thomas Nilsson; 97 (RT), Michael W. Pendergrass /U.S. Navy/Getty Images; 98-99, Daniel Chatman; 100, "Forever Tall," 2001. Created by CITYarts, Inc. Tsipi Ben-Haim/Artistic Director in collaboration with the artists Hope Gangloff and Cason Search and New York City community youth. CITYarts, Inc.; 101, Gift in memory of the courageous firefighters from Engine 54/Ladder 4/Battalion 9 killed at the World Trade Center on September 11, 2001. Photograph Bruce M. White, 2010; 102, Lower Manhattan Development Corporation; 103, Lower Manhattan Development Corporation; 104, Lower Manhattan Development Corporation; 105, Mike Segar/Bloomberg/Getty Images; 106-107, Dennis MacDonald/Alamy; 108, Paul Colangelo/Corbis; 109, Lower Manhattan Development Corporation; 111, Lower Manhattan Development Corporation; 112-113, Francesc Torres; 114-115, bbc art + architecture, Baurmann Brooks Coersmeier, Gisela Baurmann, Sawad Brooks, and Jonas Coersmeier, Courtesy Lower Manhattan Development Corporation; 116, Sketch Daniel Libeskind, Courtesy Lower Manhattan Development Corporation; 119, James P. Blair; 120, Jeff Albertson/Corbis; 121, Bradley Campbell and Matthias Neumann; 122 (LE), Norman Lee and Michael Lewis, Courtesy LMDC; 122 (RT), Lower Manhattan Development Corporation; 123, Joseph Karadin with Hsin-Yi Wu, Courtesy LMDC; 124, Brian Strawn and Karla Sierralta, Courtesy LMDC; 125, Robert Jarvik, Courtesy LMDC; 126-127, Pierre David with Sean Corriel, Jessica Kmetovic, Courtesy LMDC; 128 (LE), Lower Manhattan Development Corporation; 128 (RT), Mike Segar/Reuters/Corbis; 129, Toshio Sasaki, Courtesy LMDC; 130-131, Toshio Sasaki, Courtesy LMDC; 132-133, Visualization by Squared Design Lab; 134, Michael Arad/Handel Architects; 136, Stan Honda/AFP/Getty Images; 137, Michael Arad/Handel Architects; 139, Ramin Talaie/Corbis; 140, Michael Arad/Handel Architects; 141, Stan Honda/AFP/Getty Images; 142, Visualization by Squared Design Lab; 143, On loan to the National September 11 Memorial & Museum by Anthony Gardner, in loving memory of Harvey Joseph Gardner III and Beverly Eckert; 144-145, Joe Woolhead; 146, Silverstein Properties; 147, Michael Arad/Handel Architects; 148, Stephen Chernin/Getty Images; 149 (LE), Christof Stache/AFP/Getty Images; 149 (RT), Lower Manhattan Development Corporation; 150, Robert Kornfeld, Jr.; 151, Joe Woolhead; 152, Amy Dreher; 153, Recovered from the World Trade Center site after September 11, 2001, courtesy of the Port Authority of New York and New Jersey. Photo by Jin S. Lee; 154-155, Visualization by Squared Design Lab; 156-157, Joe Woolhead; 158, Robert Kornfeld, Jr.; 160, Amy Dreher; 161, Joe Woolhead; 162, Courtesy Lee Ielpi; 163, Handel Architects; 164, Amy Dreher; 165, Handel Architects; 167, Handel Architects; 170-171, Handel Architects; 173, Amy Dreher; 174 (UP), Amy Dreher; 174 (LO), Donated by Abigail Ross Goodman; 175 (UP), Courtesy John T. Vigliano, photo by Dave Van Holstein; 175 (LO), Courtesy JoAnn Langone; 176 (UP), Amy Dreher; 177 (UP), Amy Dreher; 177 (LO), Courtesy C. Lee Hanson; 181 (UP), Courtesy Denise A. Kelly; 181 (LO), Courtesy the Judge family; 182 (UP), Amy Dreher; 183, Pending gift, Port Authority of New York & New Jersey, found at the World Trade Center site; 184-185, Amy Dreher; 186-189, Amy Dreher; 190-192, Photo by Joe Woolhead; 194, Amy Dreher; 195, Amy Dreher; 196, Photo by Joe Woolhead; 198, Photo by Joe Woolhead; 199, Amy Dreher; 200, Photo by John Bartelstone; 202-203, Photo by Joe Woolhead; 204 (LE), Mark Wagner; 204 (RT), Photo by Joe Woolhead; 205, Photo by Joe Woolhead; 206, Handel Architects; 207, Amy Dreher; 208, Amy Dreher; 209, Ida Mae Astute/ABC via Getty Images; 210-211, Photo by Joe Woolhead; 213, Silverstein Properties; 214-215, Photo by Joe Woolhead; 216-217, Recovered from the World Trade Center site after September 11, 2001, courtesy of the Port Authority of New York and New Jersey. The preservation of this artifact was made possible in part by the Institute of Museum and Library Services via Save America's Treasures. Photo by Amy Dreher; 218, Recovered from the World Trade Center site after September 11, 2001, courtesy of the Port Authority of New York and New Jersey. Photo by Jin S. Lee; 220, Recovered from the World Trade Center site after September 11, 2001, courtesy of the Port Authority of New York and New Jersey. Photo by Jin S. Lee; 221, Gift of the Suarez Family in memory of Ramon Suarez. Photo by Amy Dreher; 222, Recovered from the World Trade Center site after September 11, 2001, courtesy of the Port Authority of New York and New Jersey, presented with permission of the New York City Fire Department. Photo by Jin S. Lee; 223, Presented with permission of the City of New York and the Department of Sanitation. Photo by Jin S. Lee; 225, Jin S. Lee; 226-227, Stuart Tyson; 228, Photograph by David Monderer. Photo by Amy Dreher; 229, Courtesy of the Beamer Family. Photo by Jin S. Lee; 230 (LE), Gift of 9/11 First Responders. Photo by Jin S. Lee; 230 (RT), Recovered from the World Trade Center site after September 11, 2001, courtesy of the Port Authority of New York and New Jersey. Photo by Jin S. Lee; 231, From the PAPD 9-11 Traveling Memorial. Photo by Jin S. Lee; 232, Jin S. Lee; 233, Jin S. Lee; 234-235, "Trying to Remember the Color of the Sky on That September Morning," Spencer Finch (American b. 1962), watercolor on paper. Photo by Jin S. Lee; 236, Recovered from the World Trade Center site after September 11, 2001, courtesy of the Port Authority of New York and New Jersey. The preservation of this artifact was made possible in part by the Institute of Museum and Library Services via Save America's Treasures. Photo by Amy Dreher; 237, Gift of Florence D. Jones. Photo by Matt Flynn; 238, Gift of Alison and Jefferson Crowther and family. Photo by Matt Flynn; 239, Joe Woolhead; 240-241, Jin S. Lee.

A PLACE OF REMEMBRANCE

Allison Blais and Lynn Rasic

PREPARED BY THE BOOK DIVISION

Hector Sierra, *Senior Vice President and General Manager*
Lisa Thomas, *Senior Vice President and Editorial Director*
Jonathan Halling, *Creative Director*
Marianne R. Koszorus, *Design Director*
R. Gary Colbert, *Production Director*
Jennifer A. Thornton, *Director of Managing Editorial*
Susan S. Blair, *Director of Photography*
Meredith C. Wilcox, *Director, Administration and Rights Clearance*

9/11 MEMORIAL STAFF FOR THIS BOOK

Lynn Rasic and Allison Blais, *Project Editors*
Jenna Moonan and Amy Dreher, *Photo Editors*
Kai Twanmoh, *Researcher & Caption Writer*
Liz Mazucci, *Researcher*
Noelle Lilien, *Counsel*
Jenny Pachucki and Amy Weinstein, *Oral Historians*
Meredith Davidson, Alexandra Drakakis, Adina Langer, *Researchers*
Michael Frazier, *Public Relations*
Norm Dannen, *Assistant to Photo Editor*

NATIONAL GEOGRAPHIC STAFF FOR THIS BOOK

Susan Tyler Hitchcock, *Project Editor*
John Payne, *Text Editor*
Melissa Farris, *Art Director*
Kat Irannejad, *Illustrations Editor*
Michelle Cassidy, *Editorial Assistant*
Marshall Kiker, *Associate Managing Editor*
Judith Klein, *Senior Production Editor*
Lisa A. Walker, *Production Manager*
Robert Waymouth, *Illustrations Specialist*
Katie Olsen, *Design Production Specialist*
Nicole Miller, *Design Production Assistant*
Jennifer Hoff, *Manager, Production Services*

Since 1888, the National Geographic Society has funded more than 12,000 research, exploration, and preservation projects around the world. National Geographic Partners distributes a portion of the funds it receives from your purchase to National Geographic Society to support programs including the conservation of animals and their habitats.

For more information, please call 1-800-647-5463 or write to the following address:

National Geographic Partners, LLC
1145 17th Street NW
Washington, DC 20036-4688 USA

Become a member of National Geographic and activate your benefits today at natgeo.com/jointoday.

For information about special discounts for bulk purchases, please contact National Geographic Books Special Sales: ngspecsales@ngs.org

For rights or permissions inquiries, please contact National Geographic Books Subsidiary Rights: ngbookrights@ngs.org

Wallace Miller's quotation on page 72 comes from Jere Longman, *Among the Heroes* (HarperCollins, 2002).

The Library of Congress has cataloged the 2011 edition as follows:

Blais, Allison.
 A place of remembrance : official book of the National September 11 Memorial & Museum /
Allison Blais and Lynn Rasic; foreword by Michael R. Bloomberg.
    p. cm.
  ISBN 978-1-4262-0807-2
  1. September 11 Terrorist Attacks, 2001. 2. Memorials--New York (State)--New York. 3. National September 11 Memorial & Museum (Organization) I. Rasic, Lynn. II. Title.
  HV6432.7.R37 2011
  974.7'1--dc22
                                2010051754

ISBN 978-1-4262-1610-7
Printed in the United States of America
15/RRDK-RRDML/2

More stories about 9/11 can be found on the National Geographic Channel (natgeotv.com/911) and are available on DVD at shopng.com/remember911.